LEADERSHIP FOR THE 21st CENTURY

Changing Nations Through the Power Of Serving

Ron Boehme

Foreword by
Loren Cunningham

Frontline Communications
Seattle, Washington

Published by YWAM Publishing, a division of Youth With A Mission,
P.O. Box 55787, Seattle, WA 98155

All Scripture quotations, unless noted otherwise, are from the New
King James Bible, © 1979, 1980, and 1982 by Thomas Nelson Inc.,
Nashville, Tennessee.

Typesetting by Thoburrn Press, Tyler, Texas

Printed in the United States of America.

ISBN 0-96155-348-0

To my parents,

ROBERT AND MARY BOEHME,

who, as my dad and mom,
as well as a doctor and nurse team,
first showed me the principles of
leadership through serving.

CONTENTS

AUTHOR'S PREFACE

This book about leadership did not come out of a moment of great victory in my own life. Rather, it was born out of dark moments when I experienced the pain of failure. As I stood on a lonely beach late one evening thinking about what had taken place, a desire rose up in my heart to seek to understand the essence of good leadership. From that moment, I set my heart to seek a perspective on leadership that could guide me for the rest of my life.

Out of that strong desire, a study on the elements of godly leadership was begun that led in a number of very interesting and enlightening directions. My conclusions are the focus of this book. These truths are especially important in light of the challenges that face us as we move into the twenty-first century.

There is much to learn, and this book is only one man's pursuit of truth in a given area. But out of great weakness, my heart and mind have been encouraged that good and true leadership can be learned and applied to the situations we face. I have also learned the truth of the Bible maxim, "My grace is sufficient for you, for power is perfected in weakness" (II Cor. 12:9).

In the pages of the Bible, I discovered Jesus Christ as the perfect leader. This discovery permeates all that I have written. He was the greatest leader who ever lived because He was the greatest servant who ever walked the earth.

The book is divided into two sections. The first five chapters focus on the principles of servant leadership; the second five identify some of the leadership challenges we face as we move into the twenty-first century. The final chapter centers around the perfect servant leadership of Jesus Christ and the need for all of us to follow His example. At the close of each chapter are questions and points of application that may be helpful for group discussions, Bible classes, or other training courses.

I would like to thank the staff of Youth With A Mission, Washington, D.C. for going through many of the painful lessons with me that resulted in this study. Special thanks go to Loren Cunningham who gave me the original idea of the project as well as the general thrust of the book. He has given me a great example of leadership through serving over many years.

Many thanks are due to the YWAM staff in Hawaii for greatly encouraging me in this project—especially Paula Lambert who spent much time preparing the manuscript (a number of times). I am deeply grateful to the Morrison Gravel Company for providing the lap-top computer that allowed me to finish this manuscript while traveling. Special thanks to Joe Portale who encouraged me to expand my thinking and look into a broader historical perspective on the subject of influencing nations.

I would also like to thank my father, Robert Boehme, as well as Floyd McClung, Tom Sine, Victor and Sharon Porlier, Jimmy Draper, Dick Halverson, Jeff Fountain, Bob Mumford, Myron Augsburger, Jay Grimstead, Bob Dugan, Tim LaHaye, Gary North, Bob Weiner, and a number of Youth With A Mission leaders from around the world, who helped in reviewing the manuscript and making valuable suggestions and corrections. The book could not have been put into its final form without their valuable insight and counsel. Many thanks are due to Jim and Janice Rogers, Jim Shaw, Tom Bragg, and Jim Waller of Frontline Communications for their gracious assistance in publishing the book.

And finally, I would like to acknowledge my wife, Shirley, who as my loving companion and friend has shared with me both the good times and the hard times, and encouraged me lovingly into the search for maturity and truth. She also graciously handled our four young children while I huddled at the word processor for days!

May the result be a blessing for all who are leaders, aspiring leaders, or are aware of the desperate need for righteous leadership as we stand on the threshold of the twenty-first century.

Ron Boehme
January 1989

FOREWORD

by Loren Cunningham

Perhaps the most neglected teaching of Jesus was that of foot washing. Jesus gave us a concrete example of what it means to be a leader, and yet the world and the Church ignore it. We are experiencing a crisis of leadership and are watching as our society is quite literally disintegrating. We must hear what Jesus is saying—He is challenging us to pick up the basin and towel and serve entire nations. This is the hinge point for future history. Will we obey Him and His command to disciple all nations, or will we unwittingly aid His enemy?

Ron Boehme has done a fine job of balancing the scope of God's offer for us to learn to rule and reign with Him with the equally important concept of submission to Jesus' lordship in every sphere. This book should serve as a compass for many footwashing world-changers.

> Loren Cunningham
> Kailua-Kona, Hawaii
> January 1989

The Spirit stands for progress; and evil then, by definition, is that which refuses progress.

Origen

INTRODUCTION

In 1980 my wife and I moved to Washington, D.C. where we became deeply involved in Christian work. In the midst of all the events and activities it became vividly clear to us that in this city of power and influence there was quite a struggle going on for the leadership of the United States.

The 1980 election saw the evangelical church move into this fray for national leadership. Following the disappointment of the Carter administration, the sleeping giant of the American church began to rub her eyes, look around the national political landscape, and move into action. As a Christian, I applauded this call to responsibility and concern for the affairs of the nation and the world. That burden had personally led me to Washington, D.C. for the first time—in 1976—when I ventured inside the Beltway to publish a small book on the 1976 elections and its implications for the Church.[1]

Many believed that the rise of the so-called evangelical right (and the building momentum of the evangelical left) would quickly peak and soon fade away. But no such thing happened. Instead, the call of the hour coming from many directions was for godly people to rise to the occasion and assume leadership in society and the world. In the mid-1980s a movement was underway.

Though voices were being heard from many different segments of the Church, a uniform cry for righteous Christian responses to the needs of society was in the air. This call to national renewal took diverse forms. Some spoke of reformation.[2] Others were teaching on the concept of the Kingdom of God, and a greater degree of the realization of its form, authority, and power on earth.

Christian dominion became a much-debated concept and a popular expression. Some spoke of the need for justice and compassion in society. Others simply proclaimed the importance of a total world view that could lead society out of its downward spiral. From the left and the right, people were urged to get involved in responsible citizenship, life and death issues, environmental concerns, moral and family issues, and domestic and foreign policy. Many in the Church were turning from decades of apathy and defeatism to an outlook of victory, or, at the very least, faithful stewardship during difficult times.

A practical and active kingdom theology was being born—not without challenge and development, however. Howard Snyder and Daniel Runyon, in their insightful book entitled *Foresight* (a Christian version of *Megatrends*), predicted:

> We may expect a period of time when varying and even conflicting versions of a kingdom theology vie for acceptance as vehicles for explaining the Christian Gospel. . . . We do not expect or predict uniformity here. What we do think possible is a working consensus among much of the more vital and visionary sectors of the Church on a kingdom theology that is biblical and communicable. It will be able to integrate creatively and redemptively such concerns as the environment, sociopolitical and economic questions, spirituality and worship, missions and culture, evangelism and justice witness, as well as the problems of unity and diversity among Christians worldwide.[3]

That is what is happening right now in many countries around the world. A perspective on the present earthly aspects of the Kingdom of God and a desire for righteous leadership in the earth are becoming very important. This emphasis on righteous Christian leadership in societies and nations is a worldwide movement of the Holy Spirit. It is not a fad; it is a movement.

A fad is a human idea that catches on and is spread from person to person and group to group. It is short-lived due to its preoccupation with sensual or secondary things. A movement (in the Christian sense) is orchestrated by the Holy Spirit through many people simultaneously in many forms, emphases, and locales. It grows exponentially and broadens because it comes from God and is accompanied with great conviction.

A great movement of Christian concern and influence in the nations of the world has begun and will continue far into the future. At its heart is a cry for leadership in the Church and in the world. What are the reasons for this emphasis? Why is the question of leadership looming so large at this juncture in history?

There are a number of reasons:

- We are witnessing the waning of a 400-year civilization in the West. That civilization is about to be lost unless its foundations are restored. Such a return to a biblical, cultural consensus would restore ultimate meaning and purpose and once again result in stability and blessing.

- The decay of Western culture has left a leadership vacuum in the influential groupings of our society. There is not enough virtue, not enough character being produced to turn out men and women with the stature to guide the affairs of men and nations.

- We are also in a turnover of leadership from the World War generations to the post-war, baby-boom era. The first baby-boomers turned forty in 1986. For the next twenty years, their generation will assume the primary positions of leadership in all spheres of life. This changing of the guard is due both to age and the sheer numbers of the new leadership generation.

- The challenge of moving into the twenty-first century has prompted an examination of current styles of leadership in the world and the types of societies they produce. Historically, this has been typical when people anticipate moving from one century into a new one.

- Developing nations are desperately searching for the means to advance in the global community. There is a wind of freedom and democracy in the air (though this takes many forms and has many different historical roots). This search for liberty and prosperity requires leadership to produce true stability and blessing.

- The Information Age is upon us, and it will usher in an era of great change and potential for productivity and progress. The best leadership the world has ever known will be required to guide us through the greatest era of knowledge and invention yet seen by men.

- The predominant religion of the West—secular materialistic humanism—has utterly failed to guide our civilization into meaning and stability. In the wake of its bankruptcy, many are crying out for new direction.

In light of these and many other factors, a new trend has begun. According to Runyon and Snyder, "A trend is a direction or movement, a flow or a general tendency."[4] This trend is that of seeing whole nations changed and established in strength through the means of servant leadership. Its implications are staggering.

That's what this book is about—changing nations God's way, through the power of serving. Because of the suffering and problems man has produced upon the earth, our only hope is for the Creator and Sustainer of the Universe to wisely and righteously lead us into the twenty-first century. He will do this through His Church—living out the full power of the Holy Spirit in acts of service and faithful stewardship. This is the only model and style of the world's greatest leader, the Lord Jesus Christ.

In the latter part of the twentieth century, the emphasis in leadership circles will be on serving people and being stewards of the earth's resources. The global community must recognize that without God's help, His wisdom and empowering, the future is very bleak indeed. On the other hand, if Christians begin to act as the best servants and stewards the world has ever seen, entire nations will be affected through the power of the Gospel. Servant leadership is the greatest need that the world has at this hour—and the church is uniquely postured to practice it worldwide. Tom Sine comments:

> Servanthood and the kingdom are right at the center of what God is doing in history. But God's way isn't found in taking power but in giving it away. God's way isn't found in the palaces of Rome but in serving the poor in Palestine.
>
> Christ didn't come to take dominion, "but to lay down His life as a sacrifice for many." It was precisely because He accepted God's vocation as a suffering servant who gave His life for many, that God exalted Him and will establish His reign through Him.
>
> Therefore, if we are to follow this Suffering Servant and His leadership model, we aren't called to take power. Like our Lord, we need to serve, give away power, put others first, and yes, lay down our lives. Through losing our lives in this kind of selfless service, God will have an extraordinary influence for His kingdom.[5]

I believe that a worldwide reformation is possible in coming years. As in the sixteenth century, this sweeping reformation of men and nations will be led by obedient segments of the Church. In reality, it is obedience to the lordship of Jesus Christ and the moving of His Spirit that have brought us thus far. Increased obedience, seen in servant leadership in all areas of society, will bring full reformation.

There are many potholes in the road ahead. At the present moment, there is great debate—even in evangelical circles—about the meaning of Christian involvement in the affairs of nations. But in terms of history, we are quickly accelerating down a humanistic dead-end street. Our debate as Christians will have to end soon. Something will have to be done.

The opportunity for influencing entire nations and cultures through caring and serving is now here. Whether the world experiences great calamities or judgments, or whether a new boom lies in front of us—someone will rise to lead. It really doesn't matter what the exact circumstances will be; leadership is needed. This leadership must be the leadership of the Church in the true spirit and authority of Jesus Christ. Philip Greenslade says it succinctly:

> Any move towards leadership is a move towards the Lord Jesus Christ. To lead is to serve. This is our basic premise, first lesson and chief ambition. We first learn to be leaders by learning to be servants.[6]

Dr. Richard Halverson, the chaplain of the United States Senate, speaking to the next generation of leaders on the difference between God's way of leadership and man's, said:

> Greatness in the Kingdom of God is servanthood. The leader is the servant. The greatest is the servant of all.
>
> We see the opposite of this in our organizational charts which are always on the vertical plane. . . . *Under* and *over* are the big words, though they are never verbalized. But they are understood, and if anyone gets out of line, he is soon reminded of the level at which he fits. Mark records that "Jesus chose twelve and ordained them to be *with* Him . . ." (Mark 3:14). In Jesus' thinking, the big word was *with*. In human words, the big words are *over* and *under*.
>
> God gives power in order to serve . . . God grant that this generation . . . will seek to be [these kinds] of leaders.[7]

If we follow this admonition and cooperate with God, His Spirit will guide us into the greatest era of history. If we fail, most certainly we will be plunged into grossest darkness.

The choice is ours. Will the nations experience increasingly ungodly forms of domination through force, manipulation, fear, and deceit? Or will the Church rise to give leadership for the twenty-first century by caring for and serving the peoples of the earth?

PART ONE

PRINCIPLES OF LEADERSHIP

What is the principal intention of this commission; to disciple all nations, to do your utmost to make the nations Christian nations . . . to go and disciple them. Christ the Mediator is setting up a kingdom in the world, bringing the nations to be His subjects; setting up a school, bringing the nations to be His scholars; raising an army for carrying on the war against the powers of darkness; enlisting the nations of the earth under His banner. The work which the apostles had to do was to set up the Christian religion in all places, and it was an honorable work; the achievements of the mighty heroes of the world were nothing to it. They conquered the nations for themselves and made them miserable; the apostles conquered them for Christ and made them happy.[1]

Matthew Henry

ONE

MAKE DISCIPLES OF ALL NATIONS

In the summer of '77, I flew into San Francisco to spend a few hours with two middle-aged women who were historians. On the trip across town I was drenched by rain while scrambling for transportation during a city-wide taxi strike. Bedraggled and soaked to the skin, I finally arrived at their home in a quaint part of that beautiful city. Like two mother hens, my hostesses, Miss Verna Hall and Miss Rosalie Slater, ushered me into their home, gave me a towel to dry off, and fed me a delicious meal while we got acquainted.

After the food and fellowship, they showed me around their home—a stunning collection of antique furniture, breathtaking works of art, and a large personal library. In every room Verna and Rosalie taught me aspects of America's history and heritage as seen through the artifacts, writings, and memorabilia they had painstakingly collected. I was fascinated. After about 45 minutes, Verna turned and began to ask me some questions. One question I will never forget.

"Ron," she said sweetly and without apparent pretense, "can you tell me why Christian missions work in Africa, though extensive in nature, has left the majority of Africans still living in poverty under the domination of authoritarian governments?"

Taken aback, I struggled for an answer. It was true that extensive missions work had been done in many African nations. In fact, a large part of the African continent is more

Christianized than Europe. In some African countries, believers are almost the majority — and by the year 2000, it is expected that Christians will be the majority in the entire continent. Yet it is also true that most African nations are still backward in economic development, and most possess harsh, unstable governments.

Why are they still living in poverty? Why are their governments so authoritarian and cruel? I didn't have the foggiest idea. Shouldn't their Christian faith have led them into aspects of economic blessing and governmental liberty? Surely their faith should have made a difference in their lives here on earth.

I answered weakly, "I don't know." Verna did not keep me in suspense. Warmly and confidently she gave me the answer:

"The reason so many African Christians, and many other evangelized peoples of the world today are still living in poverty and under oppression," Verna explained, "is that the missionaries gave them an incomplete Gospel. They saved their souls and didn't teach them to apply their faith to every dimension of life. They didn't serve them by teaching them to make Jesus the Lord of all of life. So they left them to live under misery and cruelty."

I was stunned by her answer. An incomplete Gospel? Verna continued her motherly lecture as we moved through other rooms of the house, with Rosalie joining in from time to time. After our visit I thanked them for their graciousness and left. But something within me had become unsettled.

What was the calling of Christian missions? Hadn't Jesus commanded us to go into all the world and win souls for Him? After listening to Verna and Rosalie, that perspective seemed to be lacking in depth and perspective. Was the message of the Gospel broader than the saving of the individual soul? What *were* we called to do when Jesus sent us into the nations of the earth? After this little divine encounter, I set my heart to answer that question. An answer had to be found.

After all, I was a missionary.

Lord of the Nations

The older I get and the more time I spend in God's Word, the more comprehensive the scope of Christ's lordship appears to me. Many of us have believed Christ's salvation was limited to a small remnant of individuals who would come to the Savior. Deep in our hearts there hasn't been faith to believe that much more could happen on this darkened planet. On the other hand, we have believed that Jesus' death on the cross was the greatest, most powerful act of all history. Life conquering death. Principalities and powers defeated. The last Adam removing the curse from the first Adam.

Yet somewhere in our celebration of His glorious death and resurrection, we accepted the idea that sin is still the greater power on this earth—that the triumph of the cross does not really have the power to liberate entire tribes and nations.

But what does the Bible say?

In the second of the Psalms we read a promise the Father gave to the Son of God. He invited the Lord Jesus Christ to, "Ask of Me, and I will give You the nations for Your inheritance and the ends of the earth for Your possession."

In this prophetic passage, the Father specifically grants to His Son Jesus the power to possess the nations of the earth; not just a few individuals here and there; and not just a future kingdom where there will be no earthly nations. He gives to Him the nations of this earth. The more you consider the literal meaning of this passage, the more clear the meaning of the Great Commission in Matthew 28:18-20 becomes. Jesus said:

> All authority has been given to Me in heaven and on earth. Go therefore and make disciples of all the nations, baptizing them in the name of the Father and of the Son and of the Holy Spirit, teaching them to observe all things that I have commanded you; and lo, I am with you always, even to the end of the age.

Make disciples of all the nations. To say it another way—
disciple the nations. This is what Matthew Henry says when
he interprets this important passage: "What is the principal
intention of this commission: To disciple all nations, to do
your utmost to make the nations *Christian nations* . . . to go
and disciple them." [italics mine]

Discipling or teaching whole nations. Seeing entire nations influenced and changed through the power of the Good
News. Isaiah saw this prophetic view when he exclaimed:

> Arise, shine; for your light has come, and the glory of the
> Lord has risen upon you. For behold, darkness will cover
> the earth, and deep darkness the peoples; but the Lord
> will rise upon you, and His glory will appear upon you.
> And nations will come to your light, and kings to the
> brightness of your rising (Isa. 60:1-3 NASB).

What an expanded view of the role of the Church on
earth! God the Father has given to the Jesus the Son the nations of the earth as His possession. Following Jesus' death
and resurrection, the authority of God to claim this possession fully rested upon Him. Jesus commanded His disciples
to go out and make disciples of all the nations, teaching
them *all* that He had commanded them. The practical effect
of this would be to bring whole nations under His influence
and liberating power. It wasn't just individuals that were to
be saved. Whole nations could be enriched and set free
through the power of His victorious death and resurrection.

As I thought about this, Verna Hall's words began to
make sense. I, too, was a missionary with an incomplete
message. I had labored for individual souls but I had not believed the Scriptures that Jesus Christ was already the Lord
of the nations. I had not endeavored to teach my converts
and disciples *all* that Jesus commanded. I had preached a
weakened Gospel, and had not lifted up the teachings of
Christ in order to affect whole nations and societies.

But I wasn't alone. Great segments of the Church are
just like me. We deny the power of the cross and fail to live

out Christ's lordship. We give the nations of the earth to the evil one by default. God gave the nations to His Son. He told us to go and disciple them for Him. We have failed.

Thank God for His forgiveness and grace! God is giving us the opportunity to go and make disciples of the nations of the earth in our time. We are to assert the reality of the reign of God through Jesus Christ as accomplished on the cross of Calvary. Thomas Aquinas states:

> We confess our belief in one God and one Lord, according to the words of the Apostle (I Cor. 8:6): To us there is but one God, the Father . . . and one Lord, and both of these pertain to government. For to the Lord belongs dominion over subjects. Therefore the world is governed by one.[2]

It is time to lift up the salvation and lordship of Christ in every sphere of life, in all the nations of the world. This will be done as we win men and women to Jesus, teach them all that He commanded, and serve people as stewards of society and the earth. Our motive must be to serve. Service will bring both leadership and influence.

As we do this, whole nations and cultures will be changed through the power of the Holy Spirit. Every individual will not be saved, because that is a matter of personal choice; many will choose the broad path of destruction (Matt. 7:13). But whole tribes and countries will experience the salt and light of the awakened and caring Church. The Master Himself said:

> You are the salt of the earth; but if the salt loses its flavor, how shall it be seasoned? It is then good for nothing but to be thrown out and trampled under foot by men.

> You are the light of the world. A city that is set on a hill cannot be hidden. Nor do they take a lamp and put it under a basket, but on a lampstand, and it gives light to all who are in the house.

> Let your light so shine before men that they may see your good works and glorify your Father in heaven (Matt. 5:13-16).

The Cultural Mandate of the Gospel

As Christians live out the power of the cross and the lordship of Christ in all arenas of life, this will inevitably lead to the shaping of human culture. Ultimately, the battle for the nations of the earth will be a battle for culture.

There are basic principles that apply to all human culture. A culture makes a nation. A culture forms the boundaries and creates the distinctives of any group of people. If we are to understand what Jesus would have us do, we must understand what He wants us to do with human culture.

All culture is religious. We cannot separate culture from religion because the very essence of culture is the expressing of values or worship among a people. Ray Sutton gives an excellent definition of culture:

> There are no sacred/profane categories inherent in creation. The original garden had zones that were nearer to and further away from God, but everywhere was sacred. Corporate man, male and female, was to spread culture. What is culture? *"Culture"* comes from *cultus* meaning worship. Thus [we are] . . . to transform the world into a place of worship, and thereby create true culture. . . . [We are] making society into a proper place to worship God.[3]

The very nature of culture is to make worship. It creates societal forms that represent the values or gods of that particular group of people. These cultural expressions define a group of people and give them their identity. No culture is religiously neutral. All culture is directly or indirectly related to what a given society values.

To understand a culture is to perceive its world view, which ultimately relates to its concept of God. It expresses these values in family relationships, in religious ceremonies, in art, in labor, in dress, and in custom. All cultures have a religious foundation (including atheistic ones such as Marxism-Leninism). After all, the basic concept of religion, taken from the Latin word *re-ligare* simply means *that which one ties back to*, or the ultimate upon which one relies. A nation's culture is a developed expression of its religious moorings.

Culture is a silent way of expressing a nation's religion. It is a way of stating its beliefs without all the trappings of ceremony and form. Allan Bloom says, "The very idea of culture was a way of preserving something like religion without talking about it. Culture is a synthesis of reason and religion, attempting to hide the sharp distinction. . . . "[4] He goes on to add, "A shared sense of the sacred is the surest way to recognize a culture, and the key to understanding it and all its facets. . . . What a people bows before tells us what it is."[5]

It is not always easy to see "what a people bows before." But as you analyze any given culture in the world, you can know that you are looking at the silent voice of worship and sacredness. The values of a people are intertwined in the tapestry of the culture. Whether we look at the "youth culture," the "rock culture," the "Hindu culture," or the "Japanese culture," we can identify values by looking at their cultural expressions. People have *gods*, and their commitment to them writes the cultural language of the land.

Creating culture is what man was placed on the earth to do. God gave man the mandate to tend, rule, and cultivate the earth. Of course, God expected man to make the earth a place for the glory and worship of Him. Man was not meant to fill the world with idolatry and cause his own destruction. No. Man was given the unique privilege of taking an entire planet and transforming it into a habitation of fellowship with the living God. Since the coming of Christ to redeem fallen man, this mandate has been given the new meaning of bringing all things under the subjection of Jesus. Jon Kennedy says:

> The Bible teaches that man is responsible for culture, for bringing all of creation into subjection to Jesus Christ, through His power in us (Gen. 1:28, 29; 9:2, 3. Ps. 8. Heb. 2:5-8. Col. 1). The family, idle time, and the educational portion of one's life, political responsibility, the church

worship community, and vocation are all . . . areas in
which God is sovereign and His sons are to serve Him.
The Bible, contrary to much church teaching, never sug-
gests that the religious establishment is to stand as sovereign or mediator over these areas, but rather the church is
just one of the areas of life to be subjected to God's dominion. The Bible acts as a lamp showing the direction in
which man is to walk in each of these areas, but is not intended as a textbook on any of them. Writing the text-
books is part of man's cultivating, or cultural task.[6]

Human culture was originally designed to express the
beauty and reality of God in all His facets and splendor.
This would be seen in every area of life, and man was to do
the composing. When man fell into sin, the power to
achieve this purpose was lost. In Christ, it has been restored. The call of the Gospel is to bring the culture of the
Kingdom back into the world to transform and improve it.
In other words, it is to disciple nations and to culturally
enrich them. This is done through serving people and nations in the loving power of the Holy Spirit.

This leads to another critical point: All cultures are not
relative or equal. In our day there is a trend to egalitarian-
ism in culture. Some say that all cultures are neutral, and
should be appreciated as they are; that no cultures are more
righteous in outlook and expression. But this is no more true
than to say that all roads lead to heaven. They don't! There
is such a thing as truth. There is the true God and there are
false gods that are enshrined through human culture. Thus,
all cultures are not equal in their manifestation of truth. We
are to appreciate secondary aspects of culture (which we will
look at in a moment), but as to the central elements that
make up a culture, we cannot take the position that all gods
or concepts of God are equal. Scott Peck, a psychologist
with a great respect and appreciation for diversities in culture, relates:

> The key to community is the acceptance—in fact, the celebration—of our individual and cultural differences. Such acceptance and celebration is the key to world peace. This does not mean, however, that as we struggle toward world community we need to consider all individuals or cultures and societies equally good or mature. . . . The reality is that just as some individuals have become much more mature than others, some cultures are more or less flawed than others.[7]

Because the world does not believe in absolute truth, nor in the true and living God, it has convinced itself that all cultures are equal. It has done this as a means of justifying its denial of God. If there is no loving and righteous Creator of the universe, then humanism is right: All cultures are relative. We should never tamper with them or believe that they are in need of change. But this concept of openness to other cultures and ideas, as Allan Bloom so strikingly points out, is really the doctrine of being totally closed to truth. If everything is relative, then there is no such thing as better, right, truthful, or to use Scott Peck's word, *mature*. This is how Dr. Bloom states it:

> Openness to closedness is what we teach. It is important to emphasize that the lesson that students are drawing from their studies is simply untrue. History and the study of cultures do not teach or prove that values or cultures are relative. . . . To say that it does . . . is as absurd as to say that the diversity of points of view expressed in a college bull session proves there is no truth.[8]

No, some cultures are more righteous, or more mature than others because their values are focused on the true and living God. Their God is the true God, so their culture, or expressions of worship, are more closely aligned with truth. This cultural garment of righteousness is never perfect among a people or a nation, any more than perfection is seen in any human individual. There is also much room for diversity in cultural expressions, just as there are many differing points of theology within the Christian world view.

Jesus Christ came as a servant to change people and hence transform whole cultures. His salvation is a comprehensive salvation, only limited by the sin and unbelief of mortal men. In bringing His lordship into the sphere of the nations on earth, there will inevitably be a transformation and enrichment of all human cultures where the Gospel is preached and lived out in the power of the Holy Spirit.

Appreciating and Transforming Culture

In the work of Christian missions — bringing the Gospel to bear on the nations of the world — an important differentiation needs to be made between the primary expressions of culture in a given society and its secondary forms. The primary expressions of a culture center around the god or essential values (which is ultimately the same thing) of the people. These aspects of culture must be lovingly challenged and transformed into the values and worship of the living Christ. There can be no cultural relativism here. One cannot become a Christian without exchanging his gods and the central cultural forms that go with them for a new God and Savior, the Lord Jesus Christ. The idols must go, and all their primary cultural expressions.

This will not always be an instant transformation, but it must be viewed as an essential component of both individual and cultural sanctification. In the work of salvation, a person enters into a righteous kingdom where love and light reign, and that kingdom has the power and, yes, the *duty* to transform all the expressions of an individual and his world. A sinful culture based on false gods must be exchanged for a godly culture based on the truth of Jesus Christ. Without this commitment, the individual or group will still remain a slave to idolatry. This is the curse of missionary liberalism. It does not set the people free from the cultural bondage of sin.

On the other hand, there are many secondary aspects of culture (relating to dress, custom, art, color, music, mannerisms, or relationships) that do not directly or indirectly pay homage to another god or system in contradiction to the Bible. In fact, many cultures around the world have righteous expressions in their traditions that actually model the truths of Scripture in an unconscious way. Don Richardson refers to this in his book, *Eternity in their Hearts*, as the "witness" that God has left in every culture of His reality and greatness.[9] These aspects are not meant to be trampled over in insensitivity or with legalistic force. To do so is to promote missionary imperalism.

The true missions task of reaching whole nations and people groups is to thoroughly transform the primary foundations of culture, while at the same time thoroughly preserving and uplifting the secondary aspects of cultural expression. The bad is to be done away with as much as possible, and the good images of the Creator are to be retained. There is godly and unique beauty in all cultures in the world. There is also idolatry and wickedness interwoven into the fabric of all nations.[10]

The wise and successful missionary will learn to discern the difference between the two. That is not easy, but Christ and His Word can show us the way.

Make Disciples of All Nations

If we are to obey Christ's command, we must bring the full message of Christ's Kingdom into all the nations and cultures of the earth. We must preach the whole Gospel to the whole world. We must be the best servants the world has ever known. This does not mean that the whole world will be saved. History and experience have proven this over thousands of years: It is a remnant that is being saved. Yet this remnant is getting bigger and bigger all the time, and we must not limit God and the outpouring of His Spirit.

It is not majorities that set the agendas of nations — it is always a dedicated minority in that society. To disciple a nation will not necessarily mean that all of the people or even the majority of the people will give their hearts to Jesus Christ. But what will happen is that Christians as true salt and light will begin, through servanthood, to give direction to the values and focus of the people and culture. The power of the Christian testimony as applied to all areas of life will be accepted as the prevailing world view of the people or culture. They will mold their behavior and morals around it; they will in certain ways honor and respect God; they will apply His principles in their homes, families, vocations, schools, artistic expressions, and governments. In short, the power of the Christian Gospel will save a few and at the very least, enrich the lives of the rest.

This is exactly what happened during the time of the Protestant Reformation in Europe. Born-again Christians were never the majority. But the committed minority greatly transformed the culture of the masses by living out the power of God's truth in the full panorama of life. True Christians were only the remnant. But the Christian world view made a broad impact on the culture of many nations, and this discipling of the peoples provided a climate for Christian evangelism, righteousness in society, and also the development of the earth and its resources.

This type of cultural reformation through the full presentation of the lordship of Christ is possible in our day among many nations on earth. It has happened before, and it will happen again. It happens in every generation where the Church grabs ahold of the teachings of the Bible and dares to serve people in the true authority of Jesus. Jon Kennedy optimistically writes:

> The first-century Christians turned the world upside down. Luther and Calvin lived to see the course of history radically changed as a result of the cultural mandate to one sphere of life (the Church), and Abraham Kuyper saw the radical reformation of Dutch society in Church, state, education and communication. Although much of

what started through Kuyper's efforts has since tapered off or become lost to competing forces in twentieth century history, much still remains, and the reformational movement is growing in Canada, the United States and Europe.[11]

Where the future is even brighter is in the so-called Third World. God is pouring out His Spirit in amazing ways in Latin America, in the Pacific, in Asia, and in Africa. If believers in those nations will move in the power of the Holy Spirit and serve their people better than anyone else, then billions of people will be brought into the blessings of the Kingdom of God. They may not all be saved, but Christ's salvation will be proclaimed and demonstrated among them. It will transform their cultures, and elevate their lives.

This chapter began with a quote from Matthew Henry. He lived in a day when the Church was busy transforming culture. It was easy for him to see how the power of Jesus Christ could change a whole society because it was happening all around him. The believers of his generation dared to believe the Bible and committed themselves to being the light of their culture. They were lifting up Christ as Lord of the nations, and in response to their commitment, obedience, and faith, whole peoples were being given into the hands of the King.

Societies will either possess the blessings of Christian influence and culture, or they will produce many unpleasant fruits of idolatry and error. All nations have a choice. One religious world view has to be predominant in a culture. There is no such thing as a totally pluralistic culture. In the West, pluralism is often a clever disguise for a humanistic supremacy that relegates Christianity to a small religious ghetto. But Christ did not come to reign in a small portion of life. He came to redeem the entire world. The Bible says, "For the nation and kingdom which will not serve you shall perish, and those nations shall be utterly ruined" (Isa. 60:12). If believers do their work completely and totally, masses will come to Jesus and whole cultures will be lifted out of degradation and suffering.

In their fascinating book entitled *Foresight*, Howard Snyder and Daniel Runyon state that the Church is beginning to wake up to its global, nation-changing power. This may be the greatest hope for the history of man in the twenty-first century. They state:

> The Church and the self-perception of every genuine Christian believer will be different as we move into the twenty-first century. While provincialism certainly will continue, increasingly, Christians will understand the Church as a reality transcending any one culture, language, or ethnic tradition.[12]

This could lead to worldwide revival. It could also lead to a worldwide cultural transformation through the leavening power of the Gospel.

Keys to Reformation

If the Church is to make disciples of all the nations and teach them to observe all of Christ's commands, there are a few things that are crucial.

First, we must preach the Gospel to every creature (Mark 16:15), giving every man, woman, and child on earth the opportunity to make a personal decision to receive Jesus Christ as Lord and Savior (John 1:12). The Great Commission is the last, unfulfilled commandment. Each convert must be trained to be a multiplying, nation-changing disciple.

Second, we must be committed to serving the peoples of the earth as Jesus Himself would. The key to changing a nation is leadership, and true leadership is exercised through serving. If Christians will serve people in all dimensions of society, then through serving, believers will give leadership to entire nations and cultures. It is the unique aspect of true Christianity: being empowered by the humility and servanthood of the Godhead, and its perfect expression in the Lord

Jesus Christ, to go forth and bring redemption to the earth through a servant-oriented Gospel.

Third, we must be convinced of the lordship of Jesus Christ. This is an extremely important point. We must believe that He truly possesses right now all authority in heaven and on earth (Matt. 28:19). We must realize He desires that the will of God be done on the earth just as it is being done in heaven. The retreat or advance of Christianity is always proportionate to the view that we have of Jesus. If we see Him in His fullness, then the world will see His reality being lived out through our lives, and will be transformed by the power of His matchless life.

Fourth, we must return to the whole Bible as our source book of all truth and of life. Revival and reformation come through obedience to God. Obedience is learned through the Word of God. The return of the saints to the supremacy of God's Word was the basis for every awakening and national reformation in history. Only the Word of God and the work of the Holy Spirit have the power to enlighten and empower us. The Great Reformation so clearly reveals this: As God's Word again made its way into the lives of everyday men and women, they began to go forth in God's supernatural power to conquer all the works of darkness. Whole nations were transformed and a Christian civilization was revitalized.

Fifth, in the underdeveloped nations of the world, we must demonstrate the Good News of Jesus Christ by ministering to the poor and to the needy. Love always cares and serves. One of its chief motives is to alleviate suffering. Its follow-through is to build or rebuild cultural foundations. This is simply a mirror image of the way God deals with us as individuals. First He stoops to care and to forgive, and then He continues on in the building process of holiness. If we do not serve people out of love for Christ, someone else will step into the void and gain allegiance. Those who serve are worthy of leadership. Those who lead will form the cultures of nations.

Sixth, we must be stewards of the earth in economic development and environmental concern. Christians have a reason to care for God's earth, for they understand the original mandate that man was given by God in the Garden. It is also true that only the Christian world view can ever create lasting progress and growth in the economic realm. It is the only world view that is true and carries the promises of both development and stewardship of the world's resources. Christians must teach their converts how to apply the Bible to agriculture, to business, to education, and to government. They must be taught to plan for the future. No other religion can promise success: Christianity can, and thus has the inside track at the developing world.

And finally, we must be men and women with Christlike character who have zeal and vision for the future. The servant leadership of Jesus, seen and demonstrated in His people, will put away all fears of religious tyranny and coercion. God did not send us to destroy the world, but to serve it in the same spirit as His beloved Son. We must come out of our prayer times and study of the Word as a people with courage and a message of hope. The world can be changed! Nations can be reformed! If we do not believe it, then leadership and societal transformation will take place in the world through those whose religion will allow them to do so. Will it be the Moslems? Will it be the communists? Why can't it be the Church, moving in the spirit and the methods of Jesus, the Servant King?

A Vision For Christ's Lordship in the Nations

All over the earth, people are beginning to glimpse new hope for the future. Despite the gathering storm clouds of darkness and judgment, many leaders in the Body of Christ now believe that we may also be on the verge of a great world revival, and that this revival could bring major reformation to whole countries and peoples. Could world revival come to the nations of the earth? If it did, what might it look like? For just one moment, allow yourself to dream. . . .

The world revival had begun. It was among the aimless and dissatisfied youth that the first awakenings took place. Large evangelistic meetings in Amsterdam, London, Munich, and Stockholm were signals of a complete turn-around for Europe. Soon people from all walks of life, from housewives to businessmen, were showing a renewed interest in prayer and a desire to rebuild and improve upon the foundations of a prior Christian culture. The threat of Soviet aggression and nuclear exchange caused the governments of Free Europe to move cautiously during the seventies and early eighties, but the awakening that began in the latter part of the decade sent a jolt of energy from Finland to Spain and back through the Iron Curtain. With new-found hope, and under the sanction of *perestroika* and *glasnost*, a number of Eastern European nations began to move away from the Sovict orbit.

Poland was the first to be freed, but the remaining countries opened up in rapid succession. There were minor skirmishes, but the Soviet Union's empire began to unravel as prayer pushed back spiritual principalities and powers that held nations in bondage for decades. Churches enlarged, and new ones sprang up overnight in Bulgaria, Hungary, and even in Albania. In the USSR, ethnic unrest in the western and southern provinces gave way to democratic reforms, allowing a wave of evangelization to sweep across most of the soviet states from Leningrad to Vladivostok.

By the mid-1990s a great change was underway across most of the African continent. So many tribes and peoples were coming to Christ, from Ivory Coast to Uganda, from Ethiopia and Kenya to Namibia, that the continent was rapidly becoming Christian. This incredible awakening produced a hunger for God's Word that led to many educational and relief projects, a new generation of African leaders that challenged their people to transform their nations with godly principles. Apartheid vanished in South Africa as blacks, coloreds, and whites came together in reconciliation and prayer that eventually led to governmental change. Soon the African Churches, which had once been the world's mission field, began to send laborers into needier regions of the globe. The more they gave, the more this fertile continent began to show the blessings of the Gospel.

By 1995 in America, an economic upheaval in the United States had brought a once proud nation to its knees. The deteriorating social climate, from drugs to AIDS, from poverty to the breakdown of the families, had spawned many movements of prayer that brought awakening to the nation. The revival was breathtaking in the nation's prisons, where overcrowding and despair led to an outpouring of God's Spirit. In the inner cities, believers were banding together to pray and rebuild their neighborhoods. Large black and Hispanic communities were leading the way in Washington, D.C., Chicago, Detroit, Miami, Los Angeles and Memphis. "Freedom Rallies," as they were called, took place in the mid-nineties under the direction of several prominent black evangelists. The same challenge was heard from Harlem to Watts: "Look beyond yourselves to the world!" The effects of those crusades were staggering: well over 100,000 blacks from the U.S. went to the mission field between 1995 and 2020.

In the Americas, one of the brightest jewels to emerge was the nation of Mexico. After centuries of economic rape, an awakening in the Catholic Church helped to place Bibles in every home in the country in the mid-1990s. This led to an economic revolution as the Mexican people resolved to live out Christ's teachings. This led to a new constitution, land reform, and a determination and creativity to establish a godly foundation for their country.

Nowhere was the desire for freedom stronger than in Central and South America in the late nineties. . . . As one Bolivian official put it: "We in Latin America have had our fill of corruption and tyrants." By 1995, Latin culture was crackling with this conviction. It was a time of throwing off old traditions, and looking forward to social transformation in the bright new century. South American crusades had a particular impact on the world community as a whole. By 1998, when breakthroughs in video technology allowed over seven hundred million homes to link up with tele-systems, the Santiago and Rio de Janeiro meetings were broadcast to record audiences. Those meetings, in which over twenty million locals were involved, were marked by supernatural occurrences. The entire world was watching when several Brazilian children who had been killed in a bus accident on the way to the crusade grounds were raised from the dead after a local minister prayed for them. . . . It became apparent that God had done the same miracle for Brazil — as well as for other nations of South America. He had brought to life what had been dead for centuries.

But of all the dizzying changes that took place on Planet Earth before the turn of the century, none was more dramatic than what occurred in the nations of Asia. The winds of change in the Communist Bloc weakened insurgents in the Philippines and Vietnam. Even though the tele-systems had not been available in China, news of what was happening around the world sparked the Great Reforms of '96 and '97. Chinese officials invited Western ambassadors and teachers to come introduce free economic development and representative government.

Meanwhile, China seemed to be suddenly swallowed by its own home Church movement — which had been quietly at work since the 1970s. Though there had been intense persecution in certain regions, the movement could not be stemmed. It had affected too many leaders in provincial governments. By the time laws were passed to permit the building of churches, local pastors realized ordinary buildings could not hold the congregations. Sports arenas were the only meeting places large enough. A great influx of trained missionaries, mostly from South Korea, Indonesia, and Japan, converged on China during the last four years of the century at the request of the Chinese Churches. By this time the nation desperately needed pastors and teachers to solve its crisis of leadership.

All over the Pacific Basin, the trends were the same. Evangelism explosions and concerts of prayer were producing democratic reforms and vast economic development. Some of the islands in the Pacific, such as Tonga and the Solomons, served as striking new models of Christian culture and community, especially through agriculture, education, and the arts. Soon the Pacific and Asia region became the dominant force in world missions as hundreds of thousands of Chinese, Japanese, Korean, Filipino, Indian, Australian, and New Zealand missionaries began to go forth from this hotbed of spiritual and technological growth.

For Christians in the year 2000, the earth had truly entered a new era. This was especially true for the people of Asia. Even though isolated tyranny existed in what remained of the Soviet Union and in the most rigid Islamic states, the earth had undergone more changes in those few preceding years than in any other period of history. International terrorism had not been eradicated—and in many ways it became more vile and vicious as it was backed into a corner—but nothing stopped the evangelism movements. In the earliest years of the new century, Libya, Iran and Syria, were major focuses for prayer and evangelism.

By 2015, it seemed impossible to report all the rapid scientific and economic breakthroughs that took place simultaneously around the world. The cure for cancer was found. Surprising fuel deposits were discovered in such diverse places as Chad, Honduras, and Pakistan. Nations that had been the most backward twenty years earlier were doubling and redoubling their national wealth. The Third World had been transformed.

In fact, there was no longer a Third World. Because of the economic miracles that had taken place, the globe was only divided into two areas: The Free World and the Dark World. And Christians from Bombay, Hanoi and Bangkok, who had lived in that darkness themselves only a short while before, were praying for the Holy Spirit to be poured out on sections of the Middle East and Russia that were still cut off from the rapidly expanding Christian world.[13]

Quite a picture, isn't it? This is just one man's speculative scenario, which is impossible to verify in detail or scope. Yet a few years ago, I couldn't have imagined such thoughts. I just didn't have the faith to believe that something like this could happen. All I could see was darkness. My Jesus was very small.

All over the world there are people who are getting a vision for the lordship of Christ to be established in the nations. I was recently in Russia and met with the leader of an underground Church movement. God had shown him that major changes were coming in his lifetime to the Soviet Empire. He believed God would give the Church an opportunity to exercise leadership in his country.

Same tune, different nation. Many believers are hearing the sound of the marching! This is what some others see:

> Jesus taught that Christians are to be "the salt of the earth" and the "light of the world." The light is not made to be put under a bushel, but to give light for all the world to see. If the salt is no longer preserving society, then it is good for nothing but to be thrown out. Jesus instructed His followers that they were to affect and transform the society around them, to make disciples not just of a few individuals, but of entire nations. . . . Is there any reason not to expect total victory? The second chapter of Psalms exhorts, "Ask of Me, and I will surely give the nations as Thine inheritance, and the very ends of the earth as Thy possession."[14]

Only God knows what the future holds. It could be the gloom and doom of increasing darkness and judgment. Another possibility is that we will see spiritual awakening and increasing judgment happening simultaneously. But it's also possible that God will give His Church an opportunity through the power of serving to lift up His lordship in all the nations of the earth.

How *big* is Jesus in this life on planet earth? Can the nations really be changed through the power of His teachings?

Only He knows for sure. As for me—I'd like to give my life trying to find out.

For Thought and Application

1. What is your concept of the lordship of Christ? Is He Lord of the nations of the earth? What does this mean? What should it mean to your prayer life and activities?

2. If Jesus right now possesses all authority in heaven and on earth (Matt. 28:19), what more authority will He have at the Second Coming?

3. In making disciples of all nations, what should they be taught that Jesus commanded? How can Christian missionaries balance the need to both transform and appreciate different human cultures? What people group or culture can you reach out to serve? What will it look like when touched by the power of the Gospel?

4. Begin to deepen your prayer life by interceding for the nations of the world. Pray for world revival. Act upon your prayers.

. . . The Church having lost its absolute—the Kingdom of God—is now in a welter of conflicting relativisms, all bidding for the Church's attention and loyalty. So the Church leaves a blur instead of a mark. Where Paul could say, "This one thing I do," the Church says, "These forty things I dabble in." The Church needs nothing so much as it needs a rediscovery of the absolute, the absolute of the Kingdom, that would bring life back into unity, point it to new goals, individual and collective, discover new power, the power of the Spirit, to move on to those goals, and give it nerve to face a hesitating and confused world.

We know everything about life except how to live it. We need nothing so desperately as we need something to bring life into total unity and coherence and meaning and goal. We have become ripe—dead ripe—for a rediscovery of the Kingdom of God.[1]

E. Stanley Jones

TWO

A KINGDOM
WORLD VIEW

I once saw a cartoon in which a boy and a girl were in heated conversation, each trying to convince the other of the rightness of his or her argument. After a bit the boy pointed to the girl's skirt and exclaimed, "Your presuppositions are showing!"

All that we do and believe is based on a set of presuppositions. Though most people have never taken the time to think through their assumptions, all of us operate in a world view that colors what we say, think, and do.

What is a world view, anyway? Ten years ago I did not know the meaning of the term. Even though I had unconsciously adopted a very comprehensive world view from my schooling, my friends, and my culture, I didn't realize it. As a teenager, if I had been asked what my world view was I probably would have mentioned the countries I had traveled to at that point (not many), as well my love of sports, pizza, and having a good time. I guess that was my "world view." How wrong I was.

There is renewed interest today in having a clear and integrated world view on which to base one's life. All of us *have* world views—a set of assumptions about life and what is true and important. But not many have taken time to scrutinize what their lives are philosophically built upon. Others hold elements of contradictory world views without knowing it.

This is akin to building a house without a foundation. Nobody in his right mind would do so if he surveyed the situation. What happens to a house without a good foundation? It either sinks, rots, or gets so "out of plumb" that it collapses.

Tragically, many lives are like houses without foundations. People scurry about erecting the framework, hanging sheet rock, putting in the appliances, collecting accessories for the inside—when their foundation is unknown or faulty. When the sinking or rotting comes, they throw up their hands in despair and simply go after another house . . . but again without a foundation. The cycle continues.

Many of my generation grew up in an era so volatile and fast-changing that we never took time to found our lives on a solid view of the world. The pessimism created by the world wars and materialism of the former generation gave us no hope for anything solid or comprehensive to base our lives upon. All that remained was rebellion against all types of authority. For some, there was an idealistic pursuit intertwined in the madness, but most of us didn't know where we were going, and we didn't know what we believed. We had a world view—"do your own thing" and "find self-fulfillment." But this "me generation" mentality had no depth nor thought behind it. Why should we think about what to live for? We thought we were all going to be bombed into oblivion anyway.

In the eighties and nineties, a trend is developing. It emphasizes the need of having a world view to base one's life upon. It says, "Life has meaning. Your perspective and your choices are important". This is a welcome return to deeper thought and analysis, but it will mean a battle between competing philosophies in the world arena.

Abraham Kuyper (1837-1920), the Prime Minister of the Netherlands from 1901 to 1905, and founder of the Free University in Amsterdam in 1880, was a man with a carefully formed Christian world view. He has been called the greatest evangelical thinker since Jonathan Edwards.[2] Bernard Ramm, commenting on the life of this spiritual and political leader, explained:

His [Christian faith] was not exhausted in our doctrine of salvation. It called forth the entire man, and the entire man in his cultural commitments — politics, science, art, education. His entire educational philosophy, which he built into the curriculum of the Free University, was that Christianity calls us to an entire life-perspective, a total way of living, to a *weltanschauung* [world perspective].[3]

A *weltanschauung*. A world perspective or a world view. Dr. Kuyper made a great contribution to his generation because he had a total world view and conscientiously lived it out in all areas of his life. He had a grid through which he viewed the world. We all have that. But his was carefully and prayerfully thought through and applied to the benefit of the world. He was one of the great leaders of the turn of the century both in the Church and in national government, as well as in the realm of education. Listen to his concept of the Christian life system:

> Christianity did not stop at a church order, but expanded in a life-system, and did not exhaust its energy in a dogmatical construction, but created a life- and world-view . . . able to fit itself to the needs of every stage of human development in every department of life. It raised our Christian religion to its highest spiritual splendor; it created a church order, which became the preformation of state confederation; it proved to be the guardian angel of science; it emancipated art; it propagated a political scheme, which gave birth to constitutional government, both in Europe and America; it fostered agriculture and industry, commerce and navigation; it put a thorough Christian stamp upon home-life and family-ties; it produced, through its high moral standard, purity in our social circles; and to this manifold effect it placed beneath Church and State . . . a fundamental philosophic conception strictly derived from its dominating principle, and therefore all its own.[4]

Dr. Kuyper believed that there were five basic world

views that competed for the hearts and minds of men. These were:

- the pagan or pantheistic world view
- the islamic world view
- the institutional church world view
- the modernist or humanist world view
- the biblical Christian world view

All of these world views had a distinct concept of their relationship to God, to other men, and to the physical world. (We will look at them in greater depth in Chapter 8, "The Battle For World Leadership.") With vigor and clarity of intellect, he championed the reasonableness of the biblical Christian world view. How desperately that is needed in our day!

A book that has recently revealed the deception of university education in the United States is "The Closing of the American Mind" by Dr. Allan Bloom, co-director of the John M. Olin Center for Inquiry into the Theory and Practice of Democracy at the University of Chicago. This monumental work indicts our institutes of higher education for training students to close their minds to the pursuit of truth.

Dr. Bloom says the only world view that the modern university student is encouraged to accept is one of "openness." All is relative, there is neither truth nor standards of right and wrong, of good and superior — in either men or in civilizations. He says that this openness world view has failed democracy and impoverished the souls of today's students.[5]

Men's world views *do* determine their history. They also determine, to a great extent, personal destinies within that "life-system." Consciously or unconsciously, our view of life will chart our course. A wrong world view will lead us into a wrong lifestyle. A right world view will not only lay a solid foundation for our lives, but will help us exercise good leadership.

A Christian World View

The movement toward Christians serving in society that is emerging all over the world is based on a very clear world view. This thinking is not new, it is just being rediscovered. Its rebirth could be one of the most important things happening in our time. Its application will make a profound impact on the history of man.

Certain foundational truths undergird a Christian world view. Within these truths are many shades of meaning, points of doctrine, and areas of differing interpretation. These are secondary. But the foundation stones themselves are utterly crucial. Without these basic presuppositional truths, life cannot be viewed realistically. To operate without them is to live in some degree of illusion and fantasy. They are the basic building blocks of life.

Take a few moments to meditate on these seven fundamental premises of a Christian life and world view. We will show their importance to our understanding and the consequences of our neglect to live them out.

Foundation I — God

There is one true God who is king of heaven and earth.

A beginning truth is that there is one true God. *God exists.* All concepts of life, time, space, meaning, value, and relationship come from Him. Knowing Him is the greatest joy and privilege of life (Jer. 9:23, 24, Phil. 3:8-11). God is the uncreated, triune, Creator of all that is. He has the perfect character and the ultimate authority to govern the universe, and *all* authority comes from Him (Ps. 103:19, Prov. 8:15).

Importance to our understanding: Acknowledgment of God's existence, and a deep sense of awe and respect of Him are the first steps to all wisdom. His reality gives a center point on which to focus. He gives our lives power and meaning, a reason to live and a reason to die.

Consequences of our neglect: The person who doesn't know God or acknowledge His existence is lost in mental and emotional darkness. Life is superficial, filled with loneliness, guilt, fear, and despair due to separation from the Creator. History has no direction, and sin and selfishness reign as the masters of the universe.

Our knowledge of God and His attributes is the most important reality of our life. He is the *first truth*. A person who denies His importance to the world is simply a fool (Ps. 14:1), living in great darkness and deception. The more we know Him, the more we will love and serve Him. The more we understand His power and rulership, the more we will allow it to be lived out in our lives and in the world.

Abraham Lincoln said:

It is the duty of nations, as well as men, to own their dependence upon the overruling power of God and to recognize the sublime truth announced in the Holy Scriptures and proven by all history, that those nations only are blessed whose God is the Lord.[6]

Foundation II — The Bible

The Bible is the truth about God and His world.

The clearest revelation of God and all truth is contained in the book we call the Bible. It has been hailed as the greatest book ever written. More copies have been made in more languages than any book in all of time. In the Christian world view, the Bible as the final, authoritative source of all truth is utterly foundational. It is unique in that it is the inspired and infallible Word of God (II Tim. 3:16), it is our perfect handbook for living, and as we allow the Holy Spirit to reveal it to us, it has the power to change us and human history.

Importance to our understanding: Through the Bible we get to know the true God and experience the salvation found in His Son. It gives a clear understanding of where we've come from, what we are on earth to do, and what the future holds. With the Holy Spirit illumining it, we can mold our lives, families, and societies around its teachings.

Consequences of our neglect: We will be separated from the knowledge of God and His saving power. The past, present, and future will be a confusing fog of man-made ideas. And there will be no accurate handbook for facing the decisions and situations of life.

The Bible must be our source for knowledge of God and all other questions of life. It is the Book of books. Without it, our world view has no objective foundation. Noah Webster, the father of the English dictionary, stated this clearly:

> The moral principles and precepts contained in the Scriptures ought to form the basis of all our civil constitutions and laws. All the miseries and evils which men suffer from vice, crime, ambition, injustice, oppression, slavery, and war, proceed from their despising or neglecting the precepts contained in the Bible.[7]

Foundation III — Man

Man is God's special, yet fallen creation.

To have a proper view of life, one must have a proper view of man. Man is a special creation of God, made in His image. Man is not an animal. If he thinks he is an animal, he will likely act like one, for "as a man thinks, so he is" (Prov. 23:7). Man was created in God's image; he has the abilities of intellect, emotion, conscience, imagination, and free will. He was created to share relationship with God and with others, and to be a steward over the earth. Man is also fallen and lost in sin — the object of God's special mercy and redemption.

Importance to our understanding: Knowing our special creation and responsibilities should elevate us to their fulfillment. Human life takes on great dignity, purpose, and sanctity. Knowing your design helps you fulfill your destiny. Relationship with God and others becomes the training ground for eternity. Awareness of human sin leads to dependence upon God and a proper understanding of the source of misery and suffering on earth.

Consequences of our neglect: Not perceiving our special creation can lead to the full spectrum of selfishness and animal-like behavior. Life becomes cheap and relationships shallow. Virtue is not developed through friendship with God and human potential is stifled. Not understanding the fall of man leads to human efforts toward perfection and culture building which ultimately fall apart.

Man is a uniquely created being. However, because of sin this potential for good and for stewardship of the earth has been greatly perverted. Still, God has provided a way to restore man to his original purpose. His happiness in the here-and-now and his future in eternity depend on whether he avails himself of God's gracious provision.

Foundation IV — Satan and his fallen angels

Satan and his demons are at war with man.

Satan, or Lucifer, is a fallen angel who directs an evil conspiracy from the unseen world aimed at destroying the lives and souls of men. Isaiah 14 and Ezekiel 28 are chapters that give glimpses of this powerful archangel who turned away from God due to pride and personal ambition. His rebellion was the origin of sin in the universe. He drew away a portion of the heavenly host in his schemes, and enlisted men in his disobedience against God. (Rev. 12:7-9; Gen. 3).

Importance to our understanding: Knowing there is a devil and demons gives a clearer understanding of both the origin and tactics of evil. This sheds valuable light on the struggles and temptations of life, and gives insight to overcome them. We can do spiritual warfare against primary sources of evil, and not waste our time on purely human symptoms.

Consequences of our neglect: We will place false blame for difficulties on solely human or natural sources. We will not learn to battle against principalities and powers. We will neglect the weapon of prayer. Satan's evil forces will continue to control whole nations and cultures as we impotently struggle on human fronts and fail to win the real battle.

We will not have a true perspective on the game of life if we are not aware of all of the players on the field. This is true of individuals and true of nations. You cannot win if you don't even know who your enemy is.

The enemy of the human race is the devil and his fallen angels. The battle between evil and good on the earth has a larger, unseen dimension. Satan has power, although his power is greatly limited both in space and in time. One day the devil's influence will be obliterated from the universe.

Foundation V — Morality

God's character and law are the bases of all right and wrong.

All concepts of right action are found in the being of God. God is a perfectly righteous being (Matt. 5:48). Out of the divine mind and the revelation of His values and actions come our understanding of what is right and wrong. The character of God is the perfect standard of righteousness, the measuring stick from which all actions will be judged and compared (Deut. 32:4, 5). His standard of behavior is applicable throughout the universe and for all people and nations.

Importance to our understanding: Knowing this truth gives a perfect compass for our behavior. In family and social relationships we know the conditions and boundaries that create freedom and blessing. Nations can make laws that uphold justice and also minister compassion. True liberty blossoms in societies that conform to the divine pattern.

Consequences of our neglect: Rejection of God as the basis of all right and wrong brings total confusion to individuals and nations. Every person does what is right in his own eyes. Societies become unjust, barbaric, and unmerciful. No one is safe and suffering and bondage are everywhere. The strongest rule the weak by force and fear.

God's perfectly righteous character and revealed law are the only true standards of right and wrong. His standards are reasonable, designed to promote the greatest happiness and harmony in the universe. He has revealed these standards in the hearts of every man (Rom. 1:19-20), through the written code, and in the person of Jesus Christ. This is the basis upon which all men and nations will be ultimately judged. Living a life of righteousness, through the power of the forgiving and indwelling Christ, is the means to godly leadership in the earth (this concept will be enlarged in Chapters 4 and 5).

Foundation VI—Jesus Christ

Jesus Christ is the King of kings and Lord of lords.

Though all of the foundational truths are important, this truth stands above the others—the truth concerning the life, mission, and current position of the Lord Jesus Christ. He is the central figure of all human history. He was God in the flesh (John 1:1) who lived as a perfect man on the earth (I John 3:5) and died for the sins of the world (Rom. 3:24-26). He is the perfect leader who imparts His very life and power to His followers through the Holy Spirit. He *is* the King of kings and Lord of lords (Rev. 19:15, 16).

Importance to our understanding: Knowing Jesus Christ is our only means of knowing the Father. Through Jesus' death, resurrection, and ascension, we are given grace and hope both in this life and the next. Through His Spirit we are empowered to live a godly life. Through His love and authority, all of creation can and will be redeemed. A world can be reclaimed and a universe restored to harmony and happiness.

Consequences of our neglect: In not recognizing the lordship of Christ, we will falter in sin and the effects of man's fall. We will have no hope and experience no power. Individuals will not be saved and cultures will be dominated by evil. We will give allegiance to those who bring misery and death instead of joy and fullness of life. We will not fully participate in all of creation being restored through the "revealing of the sons of God" (Rom. 8:19).

Jesus Christ has authority over all kings, presidents, prime ministers, chiefs, and other leaders in every nation of the world. This is not pseudo-authority. It is true and absolute authority. Ray Sutton says, "To the degree that the Church believes in the full authority of Christ in heaven and on earth, it will worship and submit to Him on earth."[8]

Jesus Christ is the central figure of all time and eternity. He was God Incarnate who lived out a perfect life of both manhood and servant leadership. He is the Savior and liberator of mankind from the shackles of sin and its consequences. He empowers the believer through the Holy Spirit to live a godly life. He is the King of kings and Lord of lords in heaven and on the earth.

Foundation VII—The Kingdom of God

The Kingdom of God is being established in all the earth.

As Jesus Christ is the central figure of time and eternity, so His ever-increasing kingdom is both the goal and direction of history. The Kingdom of God encompasses all beings in the heavenly realm and on earth who submit to His righteous reign. The Kingdom of God will grow to encompass all tribes, tongues, peoples, and nations (Rev. 5:9). It is the largest government in the universe, has the greatest power, possesses a loving, righteous King, and will last forever (Dan. 4:34). The fulfilling of the Great Commission is the great adventure of every generation, and will lead to the full manifestation of Christ's Kingdom.

Importance to our understanding: Seeing the Kingdom gives a focal point to our lives, families and ministries. It gives mission to the Church—a task to fulfill. It gives us our first priority (Matt. 6:33) and our final goal. It gives meaning to history, and excitement for the future. It gives us a grid through which we can view all the realities of life.

Consequences of our neglect: When we do not seek first Christ's Kingdom, our lives become filled with empty tangents and wasted years. Churches who neglect the Kingdom become ingrown, divided over peripheral things. Life no longer has meaning and history lacks purpose. Millions are left to a Christ-less eternity, and the Gospel is put under a bushel. Nations do not come to its light.

All history can be viewed as the providential development of the Kingdom of God on earth. Through the spreading of the Gospel into the nations of the earth, that Kingdom is expanding to fill the entire globe. In this great endeavor, there is a destiny for each person to fulfill. This Kingdom—*the* Kingdom—will grow and grow . . . and will endure as long as eternity looms. Dr. E. Stanley Jones so rightly states:

. . . if you have the key to the Kingdom, you find it a master-key, the key to life now and hereafter, life individual and collective. And that is important to the modern man: You have the key to relevancy in every situation. . . . So for the Church to be relevant the answer is simple: Discover the Kingdom, surrender to the Kingdom, make the Kingdom your life loyalty and your life program, then in everything and everywhere you will be relevant.[9]

Seven Foundation Stones of Truth

There are many other aspects of the Christian world view, but these seven basic realities are the vital hooks of truth on which you must hang all concepts of life. The

Scripture says, "Wisdom has built her house, she has hewn out her seven pillars" (Prov. 9:1).

Our world view is far more important than we realize. The battle for the minds of men is taking place in this very arena. Let Abraham Kuyper give us a necessary warning:

> It is self-deception, therefore, and only self-deception, when these practical and mystical Christians believe they can do without a Christian life and world-view of their own. No one can do without that. Everyone who thinks he can abandon the Christian truths, and do away with the Catechism of Reformation, lends ear unawares to the hypotheses of the modern world view and, without knowing how far he has drifted already, swears by the Catechism of Rousseau and Darwin.[10]

These seven foundational concepts are basic to the Kingdom of God. Perceiving that kingdom, and extending it into the nations of the world is the light of dawn before us as we move into the twenty-first century. If we see and understand the Kingdom, we can guide whole peoples into the blessings of its light. If we know and understand its King, we can serve people and nations exactly as He would.

So, to establish our lives on a firm foundation of truth, we need to set our hearts to:

- know God

- stand on the Bible

- know ourselves

- know our enemy

- live righteously

- acknowledge Christ's lordship

- seek first His Kingdom

and clearly understand that their are two different kingdoms, and two types of leadership.

For Thought and Application

1. What is your personal world view? How clearly does it align itself with the seven foundational pillars?

2. Which of the seven pillars of a Christian world view is weakest in your own life? How does this affect your lifestyle? What can you do to change it?

3. Why is it important for a leader to have a Kingdom world view? Will his world view affect his leadership of his family, business, or government? How?

4. Take a few hours to meditate on the seven foundations of a Christian world view. Ask God to help you seek His Kingdom. Ask Him to help you make it first in your life.

Two cities have been formed by two loves: the earthly by the love of self, even to the contempt of God; the heavenly by the love of God, even to the contempt of self. The former, in a word, glories in itself, the latter in the Lord. The one lifts up its head in its own glory; the other says to its God, "Thou art my glory and the lifter up of mine head." In the one, the princes and the nations it subdues are ruled by the love of ruling; in the other, the princes and subjects serve one another in love, the latter obeying, while the former take thought for all. The one delights in its own strength, represented in the persons of its rulers; the other says to its God, "I love Thee O Lord my strength."[1]

Augustine

THREE

TWO KINGDOMS: TWO TYPES OF LEADERSHIP

On special nights, my wife and I enjoy a good video or television program with our four young children. We choose a wholesome adventure story, and curl up together with bowls of popcorn. As the story on the screen develops, one of the younger ones jumps into my lap and asks, "Daddy, are those the bad guys?". . . ."Daddy, is he a good guy?" I explain who are wearing the "white hats" and who are wearing the "black hats." From then on, the good guys have a powerful cheering section and the bad guys get a chorus of steady boos!

Most people on earth believe that life is a struggle between good and evil. Whether you travel to the remotest tribe, or turn on the television set, you see this dualism. There is good in the world and there is evil. The world itself seems to be a battleground between the two forces.

In Western society, the popularity of the Star Wars movies brought this back into fashion after some years of "gray" stories. There was the faceless, black-clad Darth Vader and his evil Empire, trying to take over the entire universe. On the other side stood Luke Skywalker and Princess Lea, both clothed in white, operating in the good power of "the force." It was the classic battle between the good guys and the bad guys, (though some of its concepts were more rooted in pantheism than biblical Christianity).

That was a movie, but in real life, perceptions of this struggle vary greatly from group to group. There are many different standards of morality. Though all the major religions refer to this cosmic battle between good and evil, their descriptions of this battle and the prescribed remedies differ.

Does this universal acceptance of the battle between good and evil point to an underlying reality? Are there only two forces in the world? Can life be simplistically divided into the battle between two different kingdoms, and two different types of leadership?

Dualism in the Bible

The Bible is very clear on this point. It teaches there are two kingdoms — not ten, not forty, not a thousand — that are shaping the societies of men. Two kingdoms and two types of leadership. Though these kingdoms are in conflict, they are *not* of equal worth or power. One, the Kingdom of God, is ultimate; the other is based in deception and doomed to extinction. God in His absolute sovereignty uses the other for His purposes until the time of its destruction. Satan, in fact, is already defeated.

If we are to affect nations in our generation and be a force for good in the world, we must come to a precise understanding of the opposite ways of these two kingdoms. God has called us to live and operate in the one true, lasting Kingdom. We do not want to use any of the methods or attitudes of the other.

The whole Bible, from Genesis to Revelation, proclaims that there are two ways to live, two kingdoms to be a part of, two types of leadership or authority. In the beginning of human history, Adam and Eve were faced with a clear choice to obey or not obey in the Garden of Eden. In this opening narrative of history, we see for the first time the struggle between the two kingdoms, represented by Satan in the form of the serpent, and the Kingdom of God. We also see the two different leadership styles — one based on deception and manipulation, the other founded in loving influence. On earth, it all began in the Garden, but the struggle continues today.

Throughout the Old Testament, the most common words used to describe this polarization are *righteous* and *unrighteous*. In the book of Proverbs, verse after verse contrast the two. The righteous does one thing, and the unrighteous does another. The righteous have one kind of attitude, and the unrighteous (or the foolish) have another. The Old Testament gives no middle ground. A person is clearly one or the other. There are only two choices of character and behavior.

Nowhere is the contrast clearer than in the teachings of Jesus Christ. Jesus used many different analogies to explain that there are two kingdoms, two paths, two types of behavior, two types of leadership. Here are some that He talked about:

- a narrow way that leads to life, and a broad way that leads to death (Matt. 7:13,14).

- a good tree that bears good fruit, and a bad tree that bears bad fruit (Matt. 7:16-20).

- those who believe unto eternal life, and those who disbelieve unto eternal damnation (John 3:36).

- people who love darkness, and those that come to the light (John 3:19-21).

- those who do good deeds having a resurrection of life, and those who do bad deeds having a resurrection of judgment (John 5:29).

- men not being able to serve two Masters. You cannot serve God and Mammon (Matt. 6:24).

- separating the "sheep and goats" (Matt. 25:31-46).

- a house built on a rock and a house built on the sand (Matt. 7:24, 25).

- leaders that lord it over their people, and leaders that serve their people (Luke 22:25-27).

- sons of darkness and sons of light (Luke 16:8).

The examples He used are practically endless. Almost every time He opened His mouth to teach, He contrasted the differing ways of the two warring kingdoms—the Kingdom of God and the Kingdom of darkness.

The Apostle Paul carries over this emphasis into his epistles. It was deeply embedded into the mind of this dynamic saint. He heard the clear contrast the very day he met Jesus Christ for the first time—on the Damascus road. The first words Jesus spoke to him were:

> . . . Arise and stand on your feet. . . . I am sending you to open their eyes so that they may turn from darkness to light and from the dominion of Satan to God in order that they may receive forgiveness of sins and an inheritance among those who are sanctified by faith in Me (Acts 26:16-18).

From darkness to light. From the dominion of Satan to God. Yet, Paul had been a very religious man. Surely he must have been in some middle "gray" area of life and behavior. Not according to Jesus, the perfect judge of both character and destiny. Emblazoned in Paul's mind was the concept of two kingdoms, one symbolized by darkness and one symbolized by light. The head of one was Satan. The head of the other was God. There wasn't anything else—no gray areas. No wonder his later writings are permeated with these contrasting kingdoms and lifestyles (Eph. 5:8-14, I Thess. 5:4-8, Gal. 5:16-26).

The great finale is revealed in the Book of Revelation. When the new heaven and new earth are formed, those of the Kingdom of light are welcomed into the presence of God to enjoy Him forever, and those who are of darkness are sent to a destination of eternal punishment (Rev. 21:7, 8; 22:11, 14, 15).

The Scriptures have stated the truth. There is a right way to live. There is a wrong way to live. There is the righteous Kingdom of God. There is the evil kingdom of Satan. There is nothing in between. The kingdom of darkness may take many forms (there is a diabolical complexity to many forms of evil), espouse many ideologies, encompass many religions, include many lifestyles, but according to God's ultimate measuring stick of the heart, it is all the same evil kingdom. Regarding the unregenerate hearts of men, God sees things purely in black and white.

Dualism in Life

I have wondered whether this is the reason many areas of life are divided up between two sides. On a human level, these particular dualisms don't always equate with one being evil and the other being good. But the contrast is there.

In the world of government, politics often becomes the tension between two different parties, even in nations which have multiple-party systems. In the United States, there is the ongoing battle between liberals and conservatives; even so-called moderates are judged in relation to the extremes.

In the sports world, it is similar. In a football game, *two* teams line up on the field and go at one another. Can you imagine the chaos if there were three or four or five? There is something about the struggle between two opposing teams that stirs us, touching a deep chord within. Team or individual sports that pit one against the other are the most popular and draw out the greatest passion in the fans.

We've already mentioned this dualism through the cinema. What's a movie without the good guys winning over the bad guys? A meaningful story line always contrasts good and evil, the right cause and the wrong. Without this immortal struggle there is no story. Something within us says that we have not seen the fundamental reality of life.

Why *Two* Kingdoms?

With the incredible array of religions, philosophies, ideologies, world views and their resulting lifestyles on earth, how in the world could it be that there are only two kingdoms and two types of leadership?

The answer is simple. There is the true God and there is a devil. There is truth, and there is error. In a world without truth, there can be thousands of gods, philosophies and religions (as there were in ancient Greece and Rome). But because there is one true God, and because His ways embody all truth, then everything outside of Him is error. Those who practice the truth are part of His kingdom. Those who do not—whatever their reason or the form their rejection of truth takes—are part of the other kingdom. This is why the Bible is so black and white on this subject.

God designed us with the power to make choices. However, not all our choices are of the same magnitude. For all of us, there is a central choice we make—we might call it our supreme choice or ultimate motive. The Bible likens this to the very *heart* of man. There are really only two central choices: One is to submit our lives to God and live for Him and His glory. The other is to refuse to do so, and basically live according to our own self-desire in whatever form or expression that takes (including religious ones, like Paul).

Our supreme choice in life directs subsequent choices we make. If my ultimate motive is to live to glorify God, then when I decide whom I should marry, what my vocation should be, or where I should live, I will seek God for His will and obey Him. On the other hand, if I have chosen to live for myself and my own happiness supremely, then all of my major choices will come from that motivation—what *I* want.

And this continues into smaller decisions. The major decisions that I've made (based on my supreme choice), will dictate my daily actions. I will get up at a certain time, go to work, go about my day and return home based on the major decisions I've already made. These peripheral choices are not made in a vacuum. They are determined to a great extent by the previous choices that have already set the course of my life.

It is easy to see that the most important decision a person makes—his supreme choice or ultimate motive—becomes the fountain of the rest of his life decisions. There can be many aspects of his or her life that outwardly seem good. But the determining factor of character is the heart, or the supreme choice. If this is wrong, then virtually everything that follows is wrong "in heart." No wonder the Bible says that "the Lord looks at the heart" (I Sam. 16:7) and that each of us are commanded to, "Watch over your heart with all diligence, for from it flow the springs of life" (Prov. 4:23).

There is a true God and through Him there is truth. Those who believe and serve Him are part of His Kingdom of Light (I John 1:5-7). They are not perfect because they are human. But their will has been changed to live for Him, and the overall flow of their life follows this, with sin and selfishness being the exception not the rule (I John 3:6-10).

There is also the devil and his appeal to our carnal nature. Those who continue to give in to his temptations, and yield themselves to sin, are part of his kingdom of darkness (Acts 26:18). They may not appear to be outwardly evil, but the heart is wrong and so the rule of life is selfishness. Any apparent virtue is done for another reason.

The wonderful thing about being a Christian is that God in His great love and mercy has "delivered us from the domain of darkness and transferred us to the kingdom of His beloved Son" (Col. 1:13).

Now that we understand that there are two kingdoms, we can discuss the two forms of leadership that emanate from each. We will begin by looking at the leadership of the kingdom of darkness.

The Kingdom of Darkness

All kingdoms are built around the character of their leader. Satan or Lucifer is the head of the kingdom of darkness. As we saw in Chapter Two, he is a fallen angel, blinded by pride and self-exaltation. Jesus said more about his inner character:

He was a murderer from the beginning, and does not stand in the truth, because there is no truth in him. Whenever he speaks a lie, he speaks from his own nature; for he is a liar and the father of lies (John 8:44).

Out of the life of this rebellious archangel comes the leadership style of the kingdom of darkness. I am suggesting that all leadership in every sphere and government on earth that is not founded on Christ and His Word contains major elements that can be traced to the satanic kingdom. I am not saying that all non-Christian leadership is thoroughly evil in outward form. There are many other factors that make leadership actions a mixture between righteousness and un-righteousness. But the inner heart and many outward forms of ungodly leadership take on the spirit and form of the "father of the kingdom." There is a *proneness* toward un-righteous attributes of leadership. I call this type the leadership of domination.

The Leadership of Domination

Unrighteous leadership shows itself in a number of consistent forms. First of all, it is based on deception and lies. This is basic to the nature of Lucifer as described by Jesus, and true of all who follow his leadership style. To put this another way, it is not the leadership of humility and integrity. It cannot be built on this foundation, for to begin with it is living a lie by denying the glory and authority of God. Once a person lies to himself regarding the existence of God, it becomes very natural to lie to himself and to others in many other areas.

A recent *Time* magazine cover story entitled "What Ever Happened to Ethics?" discussed the lack of integrity in all areas of American life, especially among leaders in government and society. The lack of credibility of Gary Hart and Joseph Biden in the 1988 presidential race, and the moral failures of TV evangelists Jim Bakker and Jimmy Swaggart only revealed the tip of the iceberg of a nation's leadership fraught with dishonesty.

Ungodly leadership will lie to itself and to others to achieve its purposes. It is a cancer, a moral tragedy, and leaves a nation shaken and insecure.

Secondly, the leadership of domination operates to a great extent by fear. Instead of motivating by love and by hope, the unrighteous leader guides through subtle or overt threats. He himself fears exposure of his dishonesty and dreads losing his power and position, so he maintains control by producing fear in the hearts of others.

Marxist-Leninist governments are a classic example. Because of the deception and selfishness of their leaders, they enforce their rule through an elaborate system of fear. In Russia, the KGB is pervasively watching every person, and the threat of banishment to one of the gulags or psychiatric hospitals hangs over people's heads at every level of society. Instead of serving the people they rule, the tactics of fear and intimidation rule Soviet life.

Ungodly authority also resorts to manipulation to govern. Instead of leaning on the strength of character and principles of truth, ungodly leadership will "arrange the chips" to get its way. Manipulation can be very subtle. It can come in social forms, psychological forms, propaganda forms, bureaucratic forms, and the like. It is always positioning itself to accomplish its ends. It uses name-dropping and the tactic of cronyism. It is a sinister attribute of dishonesty.

It also has a low view of the sanctity of life. Jesus said of Satan that he was a "murderer from the beginning." When a leader does not have a right and loving relationship to His Creator, it is impossible for him to have a loving respect for man. If you don't love God with all your heart, you can't love your fellowman as yourself. The twentieth century will be known in history as the most barbaric and inhumane of all previous eras. From communist regimes which have slaughtered and displaced millions of human beings, to the abortion chambers of East and West, this century has seen an unparalleled soaking of the earth with innocent blood.

Leaders who professed to serve humanity have ended up destroying their own people.

Jesus, also said of Satan, "The thief does not come except to steal and to kill and to and destroy. I have come that they may have life, and that they may have it more abundantly" (John 10:10). The leadership of the kingdom of darkness is a leadership of death. It is detached from the source of life. It cannot create and protect life, it can only destroy. Its selfish interests will always collide with true human dignity and good.

And finally, the leadership of domination operates by force and control. An unrighteous leader has an insatiable appetite for control. He wants to direct, he wants to guide, but deep in the reservoir of his being is a lust to control others. He wants to be in charge, and finds it very difficult, if not impossible to step away from that position. His leadership is a reinforcement of his longing for power and status. To give it up is to give up his primary ambition in life.

Mark one thing about an unrighteous leader: He will find it very difficult to walk away from a position of leadership — even if a better man is ready to take the job. He has been blinded by his power. Often if he leaves, he will not leave alone, but will take away others with him, even dividing a kingdom. And he will resort to force to hang on to power. Marxist nations all operate this way. They force people to stay in the nation as slaves of the controlling leadership. What they fail to realize is that this admits the failure of their ideology and leadership. The greatest judgment a leader can face is for his people to leave. Erecting an Iron Curtain to keep them in only advertises the failure of the system.

The goal of unrighteous authority is domination and control, ending in slavery and even death of the people. Not all unrighteous leaders show their colors in such a vivid way. They may be more subtle, but beneath the surface is domination that governs by force. It can all be traced back to the example of Lucifer himself. Ray Allen comments:

Power . . . is perverted when used for self-gratification or the pursuit of illegitimate purposes. Abuse of power results when one . . . diverts [it] to serve self rather than the needs of those under the influence of his authority. One can abuse power by exploitation, by neglect, or by incompetence; and one can abuse power in any governing role—in the family, in the Church, in commerce, or civil government. Our sinful natures want to abuse power.[2]

But there is another kingdom with a very different King. This is the Kingdom of God with its sovereign, the Lord Jesus Christ. The principles of this Kingdom are very different. The principle of Christ's Kingdom is the leadership of servanthood. Let's look at its very different focus and methods.

The Leadership of Servanthood

We have already surveyed in Chapter Two the foundations of the Kingdom of God through a look at the Christian world view. In Scripture, God's Kingdom is known as the Kingdom of light, for He Himself "is light and in Him is no darkness at all" (I John 1:5).

As in any sphere of authority, the territory and leadership methods take on the characteristics of the leader. In this case, the perfect righteousness and holiness of God shape a Kingdom full of light and love, established upon pillars of truth and justice. Those who join this kingdom are invited to share in the very nature of God Himself (II Peter 1:4). This should produce in them the type of authority and leadership in finite form that He Himself possesses.

The leadership of servanthood shows itself in some very reliable forms. Let's compare these to the characteristics of the leadership of domination.

Servant leadership is based on absolute truth and honesty. Righteous leadership flows from the heart of the leader who has been honest with himself about his true sinful condition, and has submitted his life to the mercy and transforming power of Jesus Christ. Openness and transparency give him the ability to be honest in all areas of life. He is able to live a life of humility and integrity as God gives him grace and guidance. He does not pretend to be someone he is not. He even boasts of his weaknesses. He knows that his real strength is found in leaning on the rock of truth.

A hopeful sign of our time is a growing conviction that all leaders — especially those in the Church and at the national level — must be men and women of integrity and truth. This is square one in the principles of righteous leadership. Without it, the life and abilities of the leader are properly suspect. As the Bible states, "The integrity of the upright will guide them, but the perversity of the unfaithful will destroy them" (Prov. 11:3). That is true of all men, and especially those who would rise to be leaders of nations.

Secondly, righteous leadership operates out of motives of love, not fear. A righteous leader truly cares for the people and wants to serve them. God is the perfect example of this in all His relations to the universe and His creatures. His love is the supreme attribute from which all His decisions and actions flow. This is why the Bible sums it up saying, "God is love" (I John 4:8).

Love always chooses the highest good of God and His truth. This necessarily involves a righteous hatred of evil and the enemies of God. Gary North explains:

> Do I not hate those who hate you, O Lord, and abhor those who rise up against you? I have nothing but hatred for them; I count them my enemies" (Ps. 139:21, 22). David was the greatest warrior in Israel's history. This was to a large degree because he hated God's enemies with a perfect hatred. The perfect love of God necessarily involves the perfect hatred of God's enemies.[3]

Loving leadership will always choose the highest good of both the individuals and the entire domain. For the individual's good, it may require gentleness and compassion or it may use rebuke and righteous anger. It depends on the state of the individual's heart. Loving leadership must also take into account the protection of the domain or kingdom. It must exercise public justice and righteousness, for without it, the realm cannot be secure. Holding justice and mercy in tension is never easy, as any parent with young children has learned. But a loving leader, whether parent or prime minister, will seek to do right, and by God's help and perfect example, will succeed.

A righteous leader constantly asks himself, "How can I best use my abilities to serve and benefit others?" He does not seek his own status or position, so he does not resort to manipulation or deceit. He wants to see others blessed. The very essence of proper leadership is the motive of servanthood.

Also, good leadership has a high view of the sanctity of human life. Because a righteous leader believes that human beings are made in the image of God, he has a deep respect for the rights and responsibilities of men. Societies are not herds to be manipulated at will. The righteous leader seeks voluntary cooperation with individuals who are each precious and priceless in the sight of God.

Republican and democratic expressions of government can only exist with righteous authority. Western nations have enjoyed freedom and other benefits because of their Christian foundations, particularly Christianity's high regard for human life. They have also been the nations that have reached out in the greatest way to the poor and the oppressed of the world. Compassion and philanthropy flow from a heart that cares for the life of the individual.

Finally, the leadership of servanthood is that of example and loving persuasion. A godly leader does not force his rule upon his people: he appeals to their hearts and minds; he sets an example by the way that he lives and moves; he serves them with his gifts and his life; and in so doing, he wins their love and respect. They follow him because they want to follow. They grant him authority by willing consent. This is the essence of the leadership of the Godhead. God never forces a man to submit to Him. He only draws him by overtures of mercy (the cross), and the influence of His righteous rule and life. This is not a controlling spirit, but a serving spirit. Righteous leaders erect no walls around their people. They only raise up gates of righteousness that beckon thinking people to "come on over."

The only area a righteous leader exercises control in is the realm of public behavior. He does this for the common good. All societies have to have laws to protect its citizens from the rebellious. A righteous authority will control evil behavior for the sake of the people, but he will never force them to stay, or alter their conscience or beliefs. He will only influence them by godly overtures. Each individual is allowed to choose his destiny—his reward or punishment.

The goal of righteous leadership is freedom and life. It seeks to lift people up and serve them. Notice how E. Stanley Jones so eloquently describes leadership of the Kingdom of God:

> There are two possible ways of revealing the nature and extent of that kingdom. One is to inaugurate it with a fanfare of physical accompaniment that would impose that rule with thunder and lightning and earthquakes which would say to quivering man: "Obey—or else." That would create not men but slaves. The other way would be for God to hide the Kingdom in the facts of nature and life and gradually reveal it as man developed sufficiently to see that Kingdom and adopt it as his own. Then in the fullness of time, when God could find a people or nation most likely to be the people or nation to accept that Kingdom and make it its own, he would overtly reveal the nature and the implications of that Kingdom . . . in human relationships. We think that God chose the second way. . . . He revealed the Kingdom in a Person.[4]

That person was the Lord Jesus Christ. He served mankind and brought the Kingdom of God into their midst to either accept or reject. Those who are of His Kingdom must follow in His steps.

The Choice is Ours

The struggle for leadership in the nations of the earth is a battle that is ultimately between two differing philosophies and methods. There are two different kingdoms, and two types of leaders. These distinctions are not always seen in shades of pure black and white, but beneath the surface, the reality is there. The Kingdom of God, growing throughout the earth, is a kingdom of light and the exercise of loving and righteous influence. The kingdom of darkness is entrenched in the hearts of those who do not know God. As they rise to leadership, their unrighteousness and spirit of control and domination will be seen and felt.

There is a warning here for those who desire to see nations changed for Christ. God *is* giving the Body of Christ an opportunity to exercise leadership in the earth. But this leadership or authority must never be done in the spirit and methods of the kingdom of darkness. Righteous leadership is the leadership of example, influence and servanthood. It has nothing to do with a spirit of control or domination.

We must not make the mistake, often done in ages past, of exercising the leadership of Christ in the methods of Satan. Christians are meant to be "the light of the world" and "the salt of the earth" (Matt. 5:13-16). This does not mean we are to bash the world with the lampshade of truth or to throw the saltshaker of righteousness at the ungodly. Some today are doing just that. But that is not the path we are to pursue. Ray Allen writes:

> The nihilistic nineteenth century German atheist, Friedrich Nietzsche, wrote the ground rules for the twentieth century's brand of dominion: "The strongest and the highest Will to Life is found in a Will to War, a Will to Power, a Will to Overpower!"
>
> Nietzsche's philosophy added to Bismarck's militarism and Darwin's abandonment of God as Creator and Lawgiver, and gave rise to Adolph Hitler, who put their ideas

about dominion into action—dominion over weaker nations, racial and ethnic groups; dominion over justice, conscience, and human decency.

Using power to elevate your self-will over that of your enemy, enslaving them, is not God's plan of dominion. . . . Only by our becoming true servants of our fellow citizens, in all institutions and walks of life—including the realm of civil government—can we establish the dominion of Christ and the cross. Any other form of dominion is simply domination misnamed; and its kinship is more closely linked with Hell than Heaven.[5]

Leadership, in this world, must become either influence through serving or domination through control. In Old Testament days, the godly leader Nehemiah stated:

. . . The former governors who were before me laid burdens on the people and took from them bread and wine besides forty shekels of silver; even their servants domineered the people. But I did not do so because of the fear of God (Neh. 5:15 NASB).

The Lord Jesus spoke of this contrast in the clearest of terms:

In this world, the kings and great men order their slaves around and their slaves have no choice but to like it. But among you, the one who serves you best will be your leader. Out in the world the Master sits at the table and is served by his servants. But not here, for I am your servant (Luke 22:25-27 Living Bible).

As followers of Christ and members of the Kingdom of God, we must cast off *all* works of darkness and exercise leadership through loving influence and example. Jonathan Edwards, one of the prominent spiritual leaders of the Great Awakening in early America said:

The visible kingdom of Satan will be overthrown, and the Kingdom of Christ set up upon the ruins of it, everywhere throughout the whole inhabitable globe.[6]

How is that done? By living out the true principles of leadership in every area of life.

For Thought and Application

1. Why do good and evil appear to be so clear-cut in the Bible and so gray in much of human life? Where does the heart motive fit in?

2. Describe both the characteristics of leadership in the kingdom of darkness and those of the kingdom of light. What are the primary differences? Why are they different?

3. Think about your own areas of leadership. Is your leadership style that of example or influence, or do you sometimes resort to control and force?

4. Write down ways in which you can lead more by influence. Ask the Holy Spirit to empower you to do so.

When one rules over men in righteousness, when he rules in the fear of God, he is like the light of morning at sunrise on a cloudless morning, like the brightness after rain that brings the grass from the earth.[1]

David

The wicked man does deceptive work, but to him who sows righteousness will be a sure reward. As righteousness leads to life, so he who pursues evil pursues it to his own death. The desire of the righteous is only good.[2]

Solomon

And it is he who will go as a forerunner before Him in the spirit and power of Elijah, to turn the hearts of the fathers back to the children, and the disobedient to the attitude of the righteous; so as to make ready a people prepared for the Lord.[3]

The Angel speaking to Zacharias

FOUR

SERVING: THE ATTITUDE OF TRUE LEADERSHIP

The Western world, to a large extent, has lost its compass. Gone are absolute standards of right and wrong. All actions are judged relatively—both personally and culturally. Much of this malaise has stemmed from Western universities. Allan Bloom laments:

> There is one thing a professor can be absolutely certain of: almost every student entering the university believes, or says he believes, that truth is relative. Relativism is necessary to openness; and this is the virtue, the only virtue, which all primary education for more than fifty years has dedicated itself to inculcating.[4]

In June of 1987, a national public figure traveled to Duke University to give the commencement address. Speaking to a similar university audience to the one Dr. Bloom described above, he said these words:

> We have actually convinced ourselves that slogans will save us. Shoot up if you must, but use a clean needle. Enjoy sex whenever and with whomever you wish, but wear a condom. No! The answer is "no." Not because it isn't cool or smart or because you might end up in jail or dying in an AIDS ward, but "no" because it's wrong, because we have spent 5,000 years as a race of rational human beings

trying to drag ourselves out of the primeval slime by searching for truth and moral absolutes. In its purest form, truth is not a polite tap on the shoulder. It is a howling reproach. What Moses brought down from Mt. Sinai were not the Ten Suggestions.[5]

Who was that national figure? A television evangelist? A modern-day prophet?

It was Ted Koppel, of ABC's "Nightline." Like Allan Bloom, he was acutely aware of a very serious moral problem in the United States and indeed, in much of the world. He said that man had taken 5,000 years to learn a very important truth: that there is right and there is wrong. Period. He was saying that this return to a belief in right and wrong was crucial to both our personal actions, as well as to our future.

He is exactly right. The greatest issue confronting individuals and nations today is what is right and what is wrong.

No truth or absolutes and no compass. No wonder we are adrift. And nowhere does this lack of moral absolutes affect us more acutely than in the area of leadership, for true leadership is based on the exercise of righteousness. As Abraham Lincoln said over one hundred years ago, it is "right that makes might." A world without right and wrong is a world without true leaders.

And that is precisely what we have today as we prepare to enter the twenty-first century. Everywhere people are saying that we are in a crisis of leadership. We lack true leaders, and many of the leaders we have are either incompetent, dishonest or corrupt. This is not only true of the West, but is even more serious in many Third World nations, where a historical lack of Christian morality has perpetuated totalitarianism, high level corruption, and constant tribal, racial, and ideological bloodletting.

Right makes might. Righteousness brings authority and leadership. If Christians are to exercise leadership as we move into the next century, it will come about through a form of righteous dominion. This is the stuff of which true leaders are made. Leadership is not power and charisma. It is the influence of a life that is serving God and people.

The authority and leadership of God is our perfect model. He is the righteous King, and this is why He reigns. His infinite attributes—His knowledge, power and majesty—are marvelous and awesome to behold, but they are not the main reason that we owe our allegiance to Him. We love Him and follow Him because of the worthiness of His absolutely holy and righteous conduct. His authority derives from His perfect righteousness and servanthood. He is worthy to lead, and we are obligated to follow.

What, then, is righteous or true leadership? How does it lead? What does it look like in practical terms? Gary DeMar, with tongue in cheek, asks the same question:

> But what is the proper definition of "righteous"? The Bible gives us the answer: *Whatever the Bible tells us.* The humanists also give us an answer: whatever the humanists tell us. Either way, we are arguing in a circle. The question is: Is it a righteous circle or a vicious circle?[6]

Let's stay out of the vicious circle and turn to look at the righteous one! The Bible *does* give us all the answers that we need.

Righteous Attitudes of Leadership

Leadership, in the sense of the biblical world view, is based on two foundations. First of all, it is a calling, given by God. It is a gift that God gives to some people to exercise as a part of their makeup and abilities. We've all exclaimed, "He's a born leader!" We meant that the person seemed to be designed by God to exercise authority and leadership. As they say in the sports world, "You can't put in what God has left out." You can't rise to lead if you haven't been given the gift to do so. Leadership gifts are a part of God's bestowal to man (Eph. 4:7-12).

This aspect of calling is especially true of the scope or sphere of a person's ministry or leadership responsibilities. It is something that is providentially given by God to fulfill His purposes in the earth. Some people are called by God to exercise authority in a town or city. Others have a scope of ministry or authority that affects a whole nation. Some have been given spheres of responsibility that touch the whole world. No one is to compare or boast in their sphere of authority. It is God-given (see II Cor. 10:12-18). No special status is given to the scope of leadership either. Rather, we are to appreciate all of God's gifts and recognize that they are apportioned by Him.

Secondly, and most importantly, authority is based on character. All people are involved in some degree of leadership (whether it is by being Mom or Dad in the home, a big brother or sister, helping a friend, managing a plant, or using a particular gift or skill). What determines whether that authority is good or bad relates to the overall character of the individual. Has the person developed a righteous character and lifestyle? Then their leadership will be righteous. Is there a major lack of godly character? Then their leadership will be weak.

The Greeks said that "character is destiny." That is true and we might add, "character is leadership." A person can be called by God to a sphere of leadership and authority, but fail due to unrighteous character. The Bible and history are full of examples of gifted people who failed in their leadership, even becoming unrighteous tyrants due to a lack of godly character.

You can't do a thing about your calling. It is providentially given and determined by God. (Of course, you wouldn't want to, either. God wisely and lovingly knows what is best for each and every one of us.) But you can do something about your character. You can cooperate with God's grace and become a righteous man or woman. If you develop righteous character, then you will exercise godly leadership in the sphere or realm that is given to you.

This is true greatness: knowing your calling, and developing the character to fulfill it.

It is also very important to realize that all leadership begins with the inner man. It starts with our heart attitudes. Attitudes and actions cannot be totally separated—all attitudes lead to actions, and no action is without motive. But for the purpose of clarity, we will look at qualities that have strong focus in the heart first, and then move to actions.

The Bible says of the ministry of John the Baptist, "It is he who will go as a forerunner before Him in the spirit and power [authority] of Elijah, to turn the hearts of the fathers back to the children, and the disobedient to the attitude of the righteous" (Luke 1:17 NASB).

The following righteous attitudes, or states of heart and mind, will allow a person to exercise leadership in their given sphere. To the degree that this attitude is full and mature, will be to the degree that leadership is exercised. This list is not meant to be exhaustive. The Bible is filled with many other qualities of godly character, the breadth of which is beyond the scope of this book.

Inner Purity

The number one quality of a godly leader is a high degree of inner purity and personal holiness. Jesus said, "Blessed are the pure in heart, for they shall see God" (Matt. 5:8). In Scripture, this quality is also referred to as the fear of the Lord. It is an attitude of holy respect and love for God, and a deep desire to be purified in the inner man from the motives and effects of sin. Joy Dawson wisely states:

> We are only as pure as our thought lives are pure. All our ministries are only as powerful as our thought lives are clean. Where we have men, women, young people, and children who have chosen to have the fear of the Lord upon them—who are asking God for it frequently and who are receiving it by faith—we have purity of minds and a basis for the Holy Spirit to release His power in the Church.[7]

Mrs. Dawson goes on to point out 39 promises in the Bible related to the fear of the Lord. Many of these relate directly to leadership.

Because of our proneness to selfishness and pride, the true leader must begin his pursuit of character with his inner being. By the power of Christ, we must "cleanse ourselves from all filthiness of the flesh and spirit, perfecting holiness in the fear of God" (II Cor. 7:1). Without inner purity of heart, our judgment and vision will be impaired. If we walk in the fear of God, we give ourselves the greatest opportunity to think and live right. Then, we'll lead right.

Purifying the heart and mind is a daily experience as the godly leader seeks to think and act righteously as God gives His revelation and light (I John 1:5-9). This is the watershed of character. Without purity, all can become darkened. A man may not always know the true state of his heart. But he can earnestly seek to know, and respond in honesty, repentance, and resolve.

Heart purity is especially needed in the area of lust and sexual sin. The 1988 presidential campaign rightly focused on the need of high standards of personal morality. A man that will habitually lust in his inner life, or even cheat on his wife, is a man with blurred judgment and an uncontrolled appetite who will cheat on the nation. It is a fundamental disqualification for leadership. The Bible says:

> Yet the righteous will hold to his way. And he who has clean hands will be stronger and stronger (Job 17:9).

An example of purity in a corrupt world is Pat Boone in the realm of entertainment. In an industry known for lust, multiple marriages, affairs, and looseness of every kind, Pat and Shirley Boone have lived as shining lights of family stability and wholesomeness. Even the media have called attention to this fact by labeling Pat "Mr. Clean." Now in an age of drugs, venereal disease, and AIDS, no one is laughing at his integrity. Many are following his lead.

Faith

To exercise true leadership, you must be a person of faith. From a Christian standpoint, it is faith (trust and reliance upon God) that opens the door to character, for faith brings the individual into relationship with the God of life. Through faith, His righteous life becomes lived out in the believer.

Biblical faith has a number of aspects to it, and all of them lead to authority and leadership.

First of all, a man or woman of faith is a person with vision. Having vision—spiritual foresight—is basic to leading. By definition, a leader is "one who goes before." This means that he "sees" further than anyone else, and leads the way in accomplishing the goal.

Secondly, to have faith is to persevere to the goal. A man or woman of faith not only has vision, but harnesses everything to endure to the end. The writer to the Hebrews described this type of faith when he said:

For you have need of endurance, so that when you have done the will of God, you may receive what was promised. For yet in a very little while, He who is coming will come, and will not delay. But My righteous one shall live by faith; and if he shrinks back, My soul has no pleasure in him. But we are not of those who shrink back to destruction, but of those who have faith to the preserving of the soul (Heb. 10:36-39 NASB).

True faith always involves perseverance. In fact, it is through chastening and endurance that faith is built and strengthened. Those who have done great things in history are those who have persevered to achieve their goals. They saw a vision and they set their course to fulfill it. Nothing deterred them. They came. They saw. They conquered . . . by faith. This faith was full of confidence, and produced the fruit of courage.

Even among non-Christians, faith-like elements produce leadership. People in the world are encouraged to believe in themselves, to be positive thinkers, to be visionary entrepreneurs who set goals for their lives and persevere to achieve them. These are biblical principles and they work. Those who have faith will always take leadership over those who have no vision nor endurance. For the Christian, faith is more than believing in oneself. It is focused on the One who has all power and thus even greater fruitfulness and success can be achieved.

Twenty-five years ago a young pastor set out to establish a church in Seoul, Korea. He lived in poverty and appeared to have little hope for success. Then God began to speak to him about setting goals for his church in faith. First he had faith for 100 people to attend. Then he believed God for 500, and then 1,000. As he learned more about God, and developed increasing faith, his goals got larger and larger.

Today, Paul Yonggi Cho pastors the largest church in the world with well over 500,000 members. In a few years he believes he will have one million. And all over the world he is recognized as a leader in evangelism, church growth, and missions.

The attitude of faith brings leadership and authority. Faith in God produces both character and lasting success.

Hope

Those who have hope and impart it always lead those who don't. Hope, or optimism in the future, is based on God's promises and righteous leadership. It has been a necessary characteristic of leadership throughout history, especially since Jesus came down to earth.

If there was one thing that Jesus Christ brought, it was hope to a dying world. That is why the Gospel is likened to "that blessed hope" that ever remains before us (Titus 2:13). Where it came to affect entire nations and cultures, it gave birth to progress. Prior to the time of Christ, most people viewed history as a continual cycle of tension between good and evil. Following the death and resurrection of Jesus, Christianity gave to the world the idea that life can be redeemed and improved. Centuries later during the time of the Reformation, this idea began to explode upon European civilization. Gary North writes:

> It was the Reformation, and especially the Puritan vision, which brought the idea of progress to the West. The Puritans believed that there is a relationship between covenantal obedience and cultural advance. This optimistic outlook was secularized by seventeenth century enlightenment thinkers and its waning in the twentieth century threatens the survival of Western humanistic civilization.[8]

Christianity blossomed during the Reformation and the subsequent planting of the Gospel in the New World because it offered the world something no other philosophy could—real hope and true optimism. Only as vital Christianity died to some degree in the West has hope been lost. The only way it will be regained is through a revival of Christian truth.

An important aspect of hope is the willingness to live and plan with long-range goals in mind. One can truly do so if he operates out of a Christian world view that believes history is linear—that progress and increased blessing are in the order of things. Modern-day capitalism was based on this premise and has its roots in a Christian view of life. John Naisbitt, the author of *Megatrends* comments:

> The leading innovative enterprises today are gaining the edge by learning to think and plan long-term. While this shift has not taken place for the majority of people or organizations, it is true of those in the vanguard. Those who learn to think long-term will have an edge over those who don't.[9]

In other words, those who have hope and dare to plan and act with the future in mind will take leadership over those who do not. Gary North says it with conviction:

> Men without hope are ripe for defeat by men who have hope.[10]

One of the reasons for the landslide Reagan elections in 1980 and 1984 was that Ronald Reagan was a man who communicated optimism and hope. Even those who disagreed with many of his policies were drawn to him because he exuded a sincere and buoyant optimism. They called him the "Teflon President." Nothing of a negative nature seemed to stick! His hope touched a chord in the hearts of people. They wanted him to be their leader.

Man and women of hope will always take leadership. Whether it is a smile in the office today or a vision for the future tomorrow—hope will always take authority over malaise and despair.

Love

True love is the reigning principle of the Kingdom of God. If we were to take all of the attributes that godly authority entails, it all could be summed up in the one word, *love.*

George Grant gives us a well-rounded definition of the leadership quality of love in his excellent book, *In the Shadow of Plenty.* He says:

> Love involves "compassion, kindness, humility, gentleness, and patience" (Col. 3:12-14). It involves single-mindedness (Phil. 2:2) . . . purity of heart, a good conscience, and a faith "unfeigned" (I Tim. 1:5) . . . diligence (II Cor. 8:7), knowledge (Phil. 1:9), service (Gal. 5:13), righteousness (II Tim. 2:22), sound judgment (Phil. 1:9), and courtesy (I Pet.3:8). Love is the royal law (James 2:8). It is the capstone of godly character (I Cor.13:13). . . . Love is a commitment, and an obligation, and a responsibility.[11]

The concept of love has been badly eroded in recent decades. Instead of standing for the totality of character and righteous commitment, it has been reduced to lust and a mushy sentimentality. Allan Bloom describes the aversion of the modern young person to the true concept of love:

Young people today are afraid of making commitments, and . . . love is commitment, and much more. Commitment is a word invented in our abstract modernity to signify the absence of any real motives in the soul for moral dedication. Commitment is gratuitous, motiveless, because the real passions are all low and selfish.[12]

Love, as a quality of leadership, will always choose the highest good of its people. This will take many shapes because love modifies its form depending on the state of the heart with which it is dealing. Jesus' life illustrated this as He showed His love for people in tender exhortation (the woman caught in adultery); friendly rebuke (the woman at the well); strong direction (the rich young ruler); open rebuke (His own disciples); and righteous indignation (the hypocritical Pharisees). All that He did was done through the motive of true and unselfishness love. But the form varied greatly.

During World War II, Corrie ten Boom helped to operate a house of refuge in Holland for Jewish people. She and her family were discovered and put in a concentration camp where both her father and sister died. When Corrie was miraculously released some months later, she was faced with the choice of whether she would exercise love and forgiveness toward those who had hurt her family. After much soul-searching, God gave her the strength to shower her enemies with love and grace. She even delivered food to those who had participated in her sister's death. As a result of her leadership of love, God gave her a global ministry of forgiveness and reconciliation. An obscure Dutch spinster had risen to leadership through the quality of love.

The person who loves will take authority by that very act. People will always be drawn to the one who lives a life of unselfish love. Lee Grady is right when he says:

God is saying to us in the 1980s that if we attempt to bring revival and reformation to our land without the power of His love energizing and directing all our efforts, we are laboring in futility. All of our works will burn up when we stand before God on the Day of Judgment if we operate by any other rule. Love must become the plumbline by which we measure every word and every action.[13]

Compassion

Compassion is a crucial quality for those who would lead. This is especially true in our day of human exploitation and suffering. True leaders into the twenty-first century will be those motivated to reach beyond their own little worlds to the suffering and hardship of the earth's poor and oppressed. We live in one of the most cruel, barbaric times in the history of man. Righteous leadership must sound a clear note of compassion towards the needy.

The word *compassion* comes from two Latin words which mean "to suffer with." It denotes the idea of coming to the level of the one in need and experiencing the pain with him. Out of a motive of true love and caring, the compassionate individual then lifts the needy gently out of the position of want and pain. Compassion is non-condescending by its very nature. It does not think of rank, position, or status. It believes in the value and integrity of the individual and is moved by love to reach out and transform.

The Christian faith has historically led the world in compassion. George Grant explains:

> Whenever and wherever the Gospel has gone out, the faithful have emphasized the priority of good works, especially works of compassion toward the needy. They have matched the message of judgment and hope with charity. Every great revival in the history of the Church, from Paul's missionary journeys to the Reformation, from Athanasius' Alexandrian outreach to America's Great Awakening, has been accompanied by an explosion of Christian care.[14]

There is no better example of the leadership of compassion than Mother Theresa of Calcutta. Honored with a Nobel

Prize for her efforts, Mother Theresa has demonstrated the importance of caring for the weak and oppressed. She never aspired to be a leader. Out of a heart of compassion, she stooped to serve. Her commitment has become a symbol of virtue in the world today. She leads by influence, by example, by her life.

Beware of those in leadership who speak of compassion but show no personal involvement. The truly compassionate will reach out. By doing so, that person will take dominion over disease, suffering, and all aspects of human need.

Justice

Another motive crucial to righteous leadership is justice or righteousness in judgment. One cannot be a good leader if there is not a disposition to deal rightly and fairly with others. Justice is a foundation stone of any godly government. Though justice requires appropriate action, it begins as an attitude of righteousness in the heart.

A righteous attitude of justice can only be established if the basis of determining values is true. Here is where the Christian world view is so important to know, understand and apply. As Gary DeMar has pointed out, for the person who believes in the reality of truth, there is only a "righteous or a vicious circle" from which to derive our values. For the Christian, this standard is the whole of God's Word. It is from the pages of the Bible that we learn of God's eternal, unchangeable standards of right and wrong. To live out these standards among men is to live in a framework of justice. Greg Bahnsen answers the question of what is the source of true justice by his excellent book, *By This Standard.* His title says it all. It is by the standard of the Bible — God's revealed laws, values, and principles — that we learn what is right and true. To implement those truths is to exercise justice. The wisdom of God's Word boldly proclaims:

Counsel is mine, and sound wisdom; I am understanding, I have strength. By me kings reign, and rulers decree justice. By me princes rule, and nobles, all the judges of the earth (Prov. 8:14-16).

To be a just leader, we first have to choose the system of justice that is truly fair to all human beings. Divine laws for living have high respect for the individual and for all of his God-given rights.

The systems of human justice in the Western world have been some of the most humane of all history. Human and civil rights have been proclaimed and expanded. Why? Because the basis for law in Western civilization came out of the Christian Reformation of the sixteenth century.

In early America, the English jurist William Blackstone commented that eighty percent of the laws contained in the U.S. Constitution and the Bill of Rights came directly from the pages of the Bible. A strong foundation of Christian values gave birth to a high level of justice and equality among men. No wonder millions of immigrants flocked to the country which promised them "liberty and justice for all."

The blatant exception to this was slavery and the lack of civil rights for black people. A hundred years after the Civil War, Dr. Martin Luther King rose to leadership in the 1960s by awakening the American conscience. His message? "Let justice roll down." Today, through his heroic efforts, there is equality before the law and greater opportunity in the marketplace for all minorities in America. The burden for justice gave rise to his effective, nation-changing leadership.

God requires those who lead to do so in the spirit of His truth and laws. In Ezekiel 45:9, 10 we are told:

Thus says the Lord God: "Enough, O princes of Israel! Remove violence and plundering, execute justice and righteousness, and stop dispossessing My people," says the Lord God. "You shall have just balances, a just ephah, and a just bath."

Psalm 106:3 declares:

Blessed are those who keep justice, and he who does righteousness at all times.

A godly leader must be just and fair. His standard of justice must be based on the principles of God's Word. Those who practice justice and righteousness will rise to lead in a world that is filled with unrighteousness, injustice, and human suffering.

Humility

In the heart of a true leader is the attitude of humility. This is his protection from the greatest danger of leadership— abuse of power. As Lord Acton once said, "Power tends to corrupt, and absolute power corrupts absolutely." Leadership is power. The only way it can remain righteous and fruitful is for power to be lightly held in the hands of humility.

Humility is not weakness. It is an honest assessment of one's own character and gifts, coupled with a sense of one's own unworthiness and sin. It is seeing yourself as you really are—viewing your life as God views it. Noah Webster gives us this definition of humility:

> Freedom from pride and arrogance; a modest estimate of one's own worth. In theology, humility consists in lowliness of mind; a deep sense of one's own unworthiness in the sight of God, self-abasement, penitence for sin, and submission to the divine will.[15]

Loren Cunningham says that God grants authority on the basis of humility. To the degree that you are humble is the degree you can be entrusted with leadership. Without humility, authority becomes dominance and control. The essence of the Gospel is God providing a way to reclaim the hearts of sinful men, and produce within them His purity and humility. In this sense, Christians are born again for leadership. Humility helps a person lead in righteousness and self-control.

The Lord Jesus Christ is the greatest example of supreme humility producing supremacy of leadership. He said about Himself in Matthew 11:28, 29 (and He said it honestly and humbly!):

Come to Me, all you who labor and are heavy-laden, and I will give you rest. Take my yoke upon you and learn from Me, for I am gentle and lowly in heart, and you will find rest for your souls.

Jesus Christ was the greatest leader that ever walked the earth. He was the greatest leader because He was the most humble person that ever appeared in human flesh. Note carefully the words of Paul in Philippians 2:5-11:

Have this attitude in yourselves which was also in Christ Jesus, who, although He existed in the form of God, did not regard equality with God a thing to be grasped, but emptied Himself, taking the form of a bond-servant, and being made in the likeness of men. And being found in appearance as a man, He humbled Himself by becoming obedient to the point of death, even death on a cross.

Therefore also God highly exalted Him, and bestowed upon Him the name which is above every name, that at the name of Jesus every knee should bow, of those who are in heaven, and on earth, and under the earth, and that every tongue should confess that Jesus Christ is Lord to the glory of God the Father. (NASB)

Jesus had the greatest humility, so now He has been given the greatest authority. This is how true leadership works, and it is the opposite of the leadership of domination. Righteous leadership is not produced by power nor strength of personality. It comes from humility. The more humble you are, the more capable you are of leading. Humble people will not abuse positions of leadership. Their heart is right, so their leadership will be righteous.

I'll never forget the first time I met Bill Gothard of the Institute in Basic Youth Conflicts. He was speaking to over 10,000 people at the convention center in Hampton, Virginia, and I had asked him a question during a break. As he responded, I pondered the authority of this man: Here was a short, unmarried Bible teacher with a high voice and only average communication skills, yet over 10,000 people had come to his seminar. He was the only speaker. Why? Such childlike humility and sincerity were evident in him that listeners hung on his every word. He spoke mostly from experience with tremendous transparency regarding his own struggles and failures. Out of his humility came a wisdom and authority that brought amazing leadership and respect.

Do you want to be a leader in your home, your job, your city, or your nation? Then take a crash course in humility, and God will exalt you to lead. If you don't, it is God who may bring about the crash (Prov. 16:18)!

Unity

One of the strengths of the Triune Godhead is the unity that emanates from their oneness. There is something about the power of unity. People working together in unity can accomplish much more than those who operate alone. The Bible teaches:

Two are better than one because they have a good return for their labor. For if either of them falls, the one will lift up his companion. But woe to the one who falls when there is not another to lift him up.

Furthermore, if two lie down together they keep warm, but how can one be warm alone? And if one can overpower him who is alone, two can resist him. A chord of three strands is not quickly torn apart (Ecc. 4:9-12 NASB).

There is great power in unity, and this authority is not simply the addition of numbers. It is the exponential multiplication that comes through unity. When people are unified, God promises:

You will chase your enemies, and they will fall before you by the sword; five of you will chase a hundred, and a hundred of you will chase ten thousand, and your enemies will fall before you (Lev. 26:7,8 NASB).

Now if you take out your calculator, you'll see that unity does not just add strength, it greatly multiplies it! A united group has an authority and strength that is difficult to stand against. And this is not simply a human phenomenon. Psalm 133 teaches that when people dwell together in unity, that is where "The Lord commanded the blessing" (Ps. 133:3 NKJV).

Robert Greenleaf spent over thirty years as an executive with one of the world's largest corporations, AT&T. As he analyzed the strength of that company, and later as consultant to other organizations, he concluded that the best type of leadership was team leadership. There, unity in decision-making and diversity of gifts make for the best possible leadership. He feels that team leadership is the wave of the future for business. It not only increases productivity, but greatly protects the corporation and all of its workers. It is unity applied to the world of commerce.[16]

The longest prayer of Jesus, recorded in the New Testament is found in John chapter 17. In it, He prayed:

That they may all be one; even as Thou, Father, art in Me and I in Thee, that they also may be in Us; that the world may believe that Thou didst send Me. And the glory that Thou hast given Me I have given to them; that they may be one, just as We are one; I in them and Thou in Me, that they may be perfected in unity, that the world may know that Thou didst send Me, and didst love them, even as Thou didst love Me (John 17:21-23).

The greatest potential power in the Body of Christ lies in unity and oneness of mind. In a world of selfishness and broken relationships, unity is a power, a novelty and an example. Jesus said that if His disciples were one, as He and the Father are One, then the entire world would be affected by the glorious Gospel. Disunity in the Church is its greatest reproach and the source of lost power and dominion. A unified Church would rise to lead the world into the knowledge of Jesus Christ. Our lack of unity is our greatest shame, and open admittance of failure to follow the teachings of Christ.

It has been a great privilege for me to work with Rev. John Gimenez of the Rock Church in Virginia Beach, Virginia on the 1980 and 1988 Washington For Jesus rallies. "Brother John" was the man God used to bring about the largest unified gathering of the Church in the history of the United States, involving hundreds of thousands of people.

He is a most unlikely hero. John is a Puerto Rican immigrant raised in Spanish Harlem in New York City. At an early age he became a drug addict and spent time in and out of prison (he still likes to show his mug shot picture from those days!) Then Jesus Christ got ahold of his life, and with his evangelist-wife Anne, he founded a thriving church on the East Coast. It was to this man, who has a deep heart for unity in the Body of Christ, that God gave the vision to bring the American church together for repentance and prayer. Because of his commitment to unity, he is now one of the leaders of the Church in the U.S.

A person who has a heart for unity and understands the true source of that unity will rise to take leadership in his or her sphere of God-given influence. A true leader is not an unsubmitted maverick. He is a team player who recognizes the need for others.

The person who does the most to promote true, godly unity in a city, state, or nation will rise to assume the greatest position of righteous leadership (though not always humanly recognized). A righteous leader thinks in terms of the power of unity. He reaches out to others and wisely blends them together. He does not manipulate—instead he helps to reconcile. Leadership and authority will follow that commitment.

Sacrifice

One who leads must always be willing to pay the price of walking out in front. To lead is to go before. Oftentimes, this trailblazing calls for great sacrifice to bring blessings to those who follow afterwards. There is no true leadership without this element of going before. Walking out front will usually mean sacrifice.

Jesus Christ is the world's greatest leader because no one in history made such a sacrifice on behalf of others. The call of His life was that of a "bleeding sacrifice." He not only did this literally when He laid down His life on Calvary, but His life prior to the cross was one of continual sacrifice to meet the needs of others.

To sacrifice is to joyfully give up one's own rights and desires and lay them down for the benefit of others. Though sacrifice is painful and often accompanied with great hardship, the heart of the giver is not focused on self but on securing lasting help for another. Sacrificial leadership sees the needs and burdens of others and willingly sets aside its own comforts for the sake of the beloved.

During World War II, Raoul Wallenberg gave up a life of ease and social status to help many Jews headed for German extermination camps. For years he lived a life of tireless sacrifice, doing all he could to hide Jews and transport them to other countries. By his loving efforts, thousands of Jews escaped the gas chambers. But his sacrifice came at a price. Because of his commitment, he was eventually exiled to Russia where it is believed that he died in prison. Thousands of people today are grateful for his sacrificial efforts.

The true leaders of history were men and women of sacrifice. From explorers to pioneers, from frontiersmen to great military leaders, from workers among the poor, to great inventors and industrialists, one thing is characteristic of their success: it didn't arrive cheaply, but was purchased through sacrifice. For those who were Christians, they followed the supreme example of the Lord Jesus Christ, who had laid His life for them. It was not difficult to do so. C. T. Studd, the great missionary to Africa summarized it well:

> If Jesus Christ were God, and gave His life for me, then no sacrifice can be too great for me to make for Him.

In Romans chapter twelve, Paul exhorts us to "Present your bodies a living sacrifice, holy, acceptable to God, which is your reasonable service" (v. 1).

The price of leadership is sacrifice. Those who lead will have to make sacrifices. Those who sacrifice will be out front as leaders.

Servanthood

If we could choose one word to summarize the righteous attitude of leadership, that word would be servanthood. To be a leader is to be a servant of other people. One cannot talk of godly authority without reference to its hallmark: the attitude of service to others. George Grant says it with crystal clarity:

> There is a fundamental principle of dominion in the Bible: dominion through service. This principle is understood well by the modern welfare state. The politicians and planners recognize that the agency that supplies charity in the name of the people will gain the allegiance of the people. So they "serve." And so they gain dominion. . . . The principle of service is the foundation of dominion.[17]

Christians should be the world's best and godliest servants. Our example, as in everything, is the Lord Jesus Himself. As we quoted in chapter three:

> In this world, the kings and great men order their slaves around, and their slaves have no choice but to like it! But among you, the one who serves you best will be your leader. Out in the world the Master sits at the table and is served by his servants. But not here! For I am your servant (Luke 22:25-27 Living Bible).

The word *serve* or *servant* is mentioned 1,452 times in the Bible. This was the attitude of Jesus and His clearest picture of leadership.

I believe that all of the righteous attitudes that we have mentioned flow out of a heart committed to serve both God and people. The motive to serve is the attitude that propels the other attributes into the benefitting of others. God is looking for people who will give leadership to the masses by being the best servants the world has ever seen. He is looking for people who will:

- serve their families for their strengthening and fulfillment.

- learn to serve their neighbors and friends by loving them as themselves.

- be servants in their jobs and in the many realms of business and industry.

- be committed to serving the poor and needy who are growing in number worldwide.

- serve their societies in all the public domains.

The world needs a vast revival of serving and caring. The self-centered ways of the Me Generation have left the world with a bleeding void. Those committed to serving will step into that void and bring healing and hope. Serving is the God-inspired leadership style that can lead us into the twenty-first century.

To lead is to serve, and to serve is to lead. A righteous leader will serve the world with attitudes that bring authority and influence. A true servant of God and others will be:

- a pure and holy servant

- a servant in vision and faith

- a servant in hope and optimism

- a compassionate and merciful servant

- a just and fair servant of others

- a humble and transparent servant

- a servant who promotes unity

- and a servant who sacrifices.

Anyone possessing these qualities would defuse any fears of their leadership. The world needs men and women who manifest Jesus' character, motive and love. They will not create a religious or ecclesiastical tyranny to replace an economic or a political one. They will guide the world into the light of righteous leadership which is noncoercive and freedom-bearing. They will exercise authority through the attitudes of the Servant King.

For Thought and Application

1. What is the number one qualification for biblical leadership? Why is this quality so important?

2. Can you remember the ten righteous attitudes of leadership? In which of them are you strongest? In which areas are you weak? What changes can you make in your lifestyle to be a better servant of others?

3. List the ten attitudes of leadership. Can you think of other people who have exercised leadership through the practice of these qualities?

4. Meditate on the one attitude of leadership that is most important to you. Think of ways that you can serve others better through this quality. Put it into practice.

The path of the righteous is level; O upright One, you make the way of the righteous smooth. When Your judgments come upon the earth, the people of the world learn righteousness. Though grace is shown to the wicked, they do not learn righteousness.[1]

Isaiah

In truth I perceive that God shows no partiality. But in every nation whoever fears Him and works righteousness is accepted by Him.[2]

Peter

Do not present your members as instruments of unrighteousness to sin, but present yourselves to God as being alive from the dead, and your members as instruments of righteousness to God. For sin shall not have dominion over you, for you are not under the law but under grace.

Do you not know that to whom you present yourselves slaves to obey, you are that one's slaves whom you obey, whether of sin to death, or of obedience to righteousness? . . . But God be thanked that though you were slaves of sin, yet you obeyed . . . and having been set free from sin, you became slaves of righteousness.[3]

Paul

FIVE

STEWARDSHIP: THE ACTION OF TRUE LEADERSHIP

We need a new type of leader today. All over the earth, people are living in increasing chaos and insecurity due to the global leadership crisis. In many nations, out-and-out tyrants rule. In some places, military and civilian coups are constantly shifting leadership. Over half the world lives under Marxist-Leninist governments, where the common people are virtual slaves. In the West, we have grown cynical about leadership—the people assume their political leaders can't be trusted.

Our rejection of the truth about right and wrong (relativism) has produced the leadership vacuum. True leadership or authority comes from righteousness, both for individuals and for nations (Prov. 14:34). A nation that abandons its belief in God's revealed truth will be a nation without good leaders. To be a true leader one must live a righteous life that others will be encouraged to follow. A lifestyle of righteousness produces respect, fruitfulness and the authority to lead.

The word righteousness originally meant "right-wiseness." It carried the idea of doing the right things wisely. A righteous leader does the right things—this means that his "content" is based on truth, on the real world—and he does these things wisely. In other words, his methods or "process" are careful and sure. He is not brilliance with a baseball bat, nor does he use method without mind.

A central theme of the Bible is righteousness because that is how we were created to live. It is what we were restored to in Christ. It is the very essence of the life of the Godhead.

Righteous Actions of Leadership

We mentioned in the previous chapter that righteousness in leadership begins with right attitudes. It is first an internal commitment and process. We said that the attitude of serving summarizes well the motives of a good leader. But leadership is also an external lifestyle. Of course, we normally think about right and wrong in terms of outward actions.

Now we will look at ten actions of leadership described by the word *stewardship*. A good leader will be a steward of time, talent, people, and material resources. These are the most visible parts of leadership—what a person *does*. The person who acts righteously as a steward is the person who will have authority. (As in the previous chapter, this list is not meant to be exhaustive.)

Walk in Obedience

To be a good leader you must first be a good follower. The person who learns to obey has developed character and is worthy to be obeyed himself. A leader, by basic definition, always "goes before." He never asks others to do what he himself is not willing to do. If you have not learned to obey God and other authorities that He has placed in your life, you will not be able to lead others into the same, stable experience. As Bob Mumford says, "Obedience brings the right to rule."

Also, obedience is definitely *learned*. Even Jesus, as the God-Man, experienced the pain of learning obedience. Hebrews 5:8 says "Though He was a Son, yet He learned obedience by the things which He suffered." And in the next verse, "And having been perfected, He became the author of eternal salvation to all who obey Him."

Jesus was the perfect leader with the greatest authority that has ever been seen on earth because he perfectly obeyed the will of God for His life (see John 4:34, 5:16-19, 17:4). His obedience was the fountain of His authority. He could ask others to follow Him because He was obediently following the will of the Father himself. His attitude was that of the fear of the Lord. His corresponding action was obedience. Joy Dawson says it so well:

> The fear of God is evidenced in our lives by instant, joyful, and whole obedience to God. That is biblical obedience. Anything else is disobedience. . . . Authority from God is released only to those whose activity originates from God and is energized by Him. Then and then only can God receive the glory. Jesus said, "I have brought you glory on earth by completing the work you gave me to do" (John 17:4, NIV). We have no spiritual authority outside obedience to God.[4]

We can relate this to raising children. During early childhood, what is the main lesson we try to teach, whether through a strong voice, a spank on the bottom or the missing of dessert? Isn't it the simple lesson of obedience? After the embrace of acceptance and love, the lesson of obedience is the first training ground of life. From the beginning we are taught the right boundaries and learn to obey. As the child grows, self-control gradually replaces this outward control. A self-controlled life emerges through obedience.

When Arthur Blessitt was a young man he worked on his father's farm doing strenuous chores and learning to obey his dad. Over the years he learned some good lessons in instant and total obedience. When he became an adult, God called him to carry a huge wooden cross all over the world. Arthur had already learned to obey, and he carried over this attribute into his new ministry. Through jungles, over mountaintops, in the midst of riots and war zones, and into the chambers of presidents of nations, Arthur Blessitt has obediently taken his cross. His influence through simple obedience has been felt all over world.

In your family relationships, in your work, in your activities and involvements, establish the lifestyle of obedience. Obedient people will have authority. Others will feel secure to follow them, and learn to obey themselves.

Trust in His Miraculous Power

In the West there has been an increasing interest in the supernatural by people of all walks of life. Some have been drawn into the occult via magic or witchcraft. Others have been taken in by the New Age movement and its dabbling with demonic spirits and the like. Why is this happening and what is its importance to our understanding of leadership?

There is an unseen world. Though many deny it, God exists and so do Satan and his fallen angels. They have powers beyond materialistic explanation. The rest of the world understands the supernatural world well; many tribes and nations daily experience the struggle between the forces of darkness and the powers of light. In the West, we have laughed at witches and goblins, and viewed their many expressions as simple superstition. But during the past few decades, we have begun to see the reality of the supernatural world. Science lacked the answers. Materialism didn't satisfy. There were too many things that we just couldn't explain.

The realm of the miraculous is very important to Christian leadership. The use of supernatural power is a demonstration of authority in the physical world. The world will look to leadership that has authority in all realms.

The Pentecostal and Charismatic movements of this century have understood this truth. Charismatic Christians have begun to exercise increasing leadership in the Christian world due to their teaching on the supernatural power of Jesus Christ. Their involvement in physical healings, and signs and wonders has been the application of Christ's authority over the physical world. The greatest church growth is among groups who believe in and experience God's supernatural power. This power is real, and is an attribute of His authority and leadership.

Lee Grady states very well the necessary focus of the Church at the end of the twentieth century:

> As we preach the Gospel, we must yield our lives to the Holy Spirit in order that the power of God can be demonstrated to the world. We must heal the sick, raise the dead, cleanse the lepers, cast out demons, and meet the needs that only the supernatural power of Christ in us can meet.[5]

To be a true Christian leader in a world of darkness and demonic power, one needs to be filled with the power of the Holy Spirit to take authority in the supernatural realm. Fullness is likeness. We must be *like* Jesus. What was He like? He healed the sick. He cast out demons. He fed the multitudes. He raised the dead. And He said to His followers:

> These signs will follow those who believe: In My Name they will cast out demons; they will speak with new tongues; they will take up serpents; and if they drink anything deadly, it will by no means hurt them; they will lay hands on the sick and they will recover (Mark 16:17, 18).

> Most assuredly, I say to you, he who believes in Me, the works that I do he will do also; and greater works than these he will do because I go to My Father (John 14:12).

The world is fascinated by the power of the demonic. Only the demonstration of the righteous power of God will conquer the enemy and bring true authority.

Is God's power operating in your life? If it's not, seek to be filled with His Spirit. As you learn to depend on the miraculous power of the living Christ, you will increasingly experience His authority over the physical world.

Use Your God-Given Talents

All human beings are uniquely gifted of God. We are each specially designed by our Creator for a certain destiny on the earth. David rightly rejoiced in the fact that:

You have formed my inward parts; You have covered me in my mother's womb. I will praise you for I am fearfully and wonderfully made; Marvelous are your works, and that my soul knows very well (Ps. 139:13, 14).

We probably don't look at ourselves in the mirror each morning and exclaim, "Oh, I'm wonderfully made!" We don't like our looks, we're unsure of our talents (and possibly envious of others), we are bored with our jobs, and we do not easily grasp that God has given each of us unique talents and abilities.

We've all been given physical and spiritual gifts that God wants us to exercise on earth. No one on earth has the same array of abilities and gifts. They are uniquely given to each one of us. The more we understand and put them into practice, the more fulfilled we will be personally and the greater will be our leadership in those areas.

One of the righteous actions that brings leadership to a person's life is simply being who he was created to be. It is a person's gift that makes room for him and brings him before great men (Prov. 18:16). It is also the secret to a fulfilled life. You will be bored if you are not using your God-given talents to glorify Him. This was the reason for your creation: to glorify God by sharing your essence and gifts with His world.

Studies consistently show that the vast majority are unhappy with their jobs. So few people really understand who they are, how they are motivated, and what they do best. Without this knowledge, they cannot make their best contribution.

Recently I read a book called *The Truth About You* by Arthur F. Miller and Ralph T. Mattson. The authors share this perspective:

Each of us—*you*—can be a so-called gifted person . . . if you identify the gifts you have been given, submit them to whatever training may be necessary, and then employ your gifts in work which requires them. These are good gifts, and if used in work appropriate for them, will yield you and those who employ you much material and personal reward.

No person has achieved success in any field of endeavor except through reliance on gifts. What is true of the individual is also true of the organization. No business or institution has built a successful service of product except as a direct result of some men and women using gifts which have been given to them. If those gifts are not present, what was a success will fail. There is no "self-made" successful man or woman. There are only people smart enough or grateful enough to be good stewards of their gifts. Discover your design.[6]

We all need to "discover our design" and then we can do the best job that is possible to do. If Christians are to give leadership to the world, then they must be the best at what they do. This cannot be done if we are doing things unsuited to us!

Millie Nelcamp of Akron, Ohio is a second cousin of mine. In the eyes of the world she may not seem significant— she has major problems coordinating her muscles and speaks with a pronounced slur. She is a spastic. But Millie has a gift from God. She can paint. Her hands do not work so well so she uses her feet! Wonderful pieces of art have been produced by the talented feet of this amazing lady. Millie has used her gift as a good steward.

In order to be good stewards, we must discover and use our gifts for God and His people. We must be the best mothers, fathers, plumbers, teachers, scientists, businessmen, artists, carpenters, writers, caterers, and the like. We must each do what we were created to do and do it well, glorifying God and benefitting others.

Work Hard

"The hand of the diligent shall rule" (Prov. 12:24). What a simple, yet profound statement. Translation: He who works smartest and hardest will lead. Most of us realize this.

Good old discipline, diligence, and elbow grease have a lot to do with leadership. In a fallen world in which it's easy to kick back and be lazy, the person who works hard at a job is likely to excel.

I learned this while in high school playing on the varsity basketball team. I had average talent, was a 6-foot shooting guard, and played on a team with a chance to win the conference title for the first time in 20 years. However, I was no superstar. I wasn't unusually gifted, so the deficit had to be made up with discipline and hard work.

I set myself a few goals: Help the school win the league championship; be named to the First Team All League squad. I had to work hard. I got up at 5 A.M. and went into the dark gym before school to dribble, work on conditioning, and shoot . . . shoot . . . shoot. In the afternoons I ran windsprints and did seemingly endless sets of "bleachers." The discipline paid off. Six months later we won the league championship, played in the state tournament, and I made First Team All League. Most importantly, I learned a lesson that I have applied to many other areas of my life: Hard work pays off. The hand of the disciplined rules.

Samuel Taylor Coleridge had a brilliant but undisciplined mind. A gifted poet, he always talked of the books that existed in his mind, but very little was ever published. He moved from project to project, always conceiving, never bringing to birth. William Barclay in referring to Coleridge said, "No one ever reached any eminence, and no one having reached it ever maintained it, without discipline."[7]

Hard work is the price of leadership. The Japanese have shown this in business, and the Koreans are not far behind. Thomas Edison lived on two to three hours sleep a night in pursuit of his scientific goals. He failed over 200 times before his invention of the electric light bulb became a reality. My own father put himself through medical school during the Depression by working the night shift at a rubber factory and getting two hours of sleep a day for years. George Grant is right when he says:

God is the One who awards power, wealth, and dominion (Deut. 8:18), and He awards it to laborers and diligent workers (Prov. 10:4). Far from being a bitter consequence of the Fall then, work is a vital aspect of God's overall purpose for man. In fact, a man can do nothing better than find satisfaction in his work (Ecc. 2:24, 3:22). . . . We were made for work. Thus, an abundance of work is a blessing. Lack of work is a curse.[8]

Do you want to excel? You can't put in what God has left out, but you can certainly harness what He has given you through diligence and hard work. Many times this will be the difference between leading and following. Labor brings leadership and many other rewards. Believers should be the hardest working people on earth. Only our unwillingness and disobedience will stop us from being so. The great Methodist leader, John Wesley said, "Religion must necessarily produce both industry and frugality, and these cannot but produce riches."

Be Charitable

Righteous leadership will always show itself in acts of compassion and practical concern for the poor and needy. We live in a fallen world of scarcity, need, injustice, and the manifold outworkings of human depravity. The person who knows his God will quickly learn of God's great love and concern for the poor and needy. Listen carefully to this passage from the Bible:

> "Shall you reign [exercise leadership] because you enclose yourself in cedar? Did not your father eat and drink, and do justice and righteousness? Then it was well with him. He judged the cause of the poor and needy; then it was well. Was not this knowing Me?" says the Lord (Jer. 22:15, 16).

What does it mean to know the Lord? The Bible says clearly that knowing God means caring about justice for the

poor and oppressed. God has a special concern for the poor
and needy. If we really know Him, we will share that concern, and our lifestyle will reflect it.

For much of this century, various Christian denominations and movements lost the two-handed approach of the
Gospel—that is, that God was concerned with the whole
man: both people's physical needs as well as their eternal
souls. Among some groups the only emphasis was to save
the soul. Among others a social gospel ignored the soul and
fed the stomach or did other practical works. Over the years
the chasm between these two groups got bigger and bigger.
Neither was right.

God has always cared about people's eternal state and
their earthly existence. His Good News is salvation from all
effects of sin. To be a true missionary one has to live out a
lifestyle of verbal evangelism and acts of mercy. True love
contains both. Men and women are not divided into spirit
and matter. They are whole and God loves them. All of them.

Christianity has given the world the greatest models of
compassion and charity. Jesus demonstrated this in His life
and ministry, and the early disciples followed His example.
Many men and women over the centuries have walked in
the same footsteps:

- Augustine (354-430 A.D.) established works of charity in
  13 cities in North Africa.

- Bernard of Clairveaux (1090-1153) established a charitable network throughout Europe.

- John Wycliffe (1329-1384) sent out many relief workers.

- Francis of Assisi (1181?-1226) was used of God to build a
  worldwide movement of compassion.

- John Calvin (1509-1564) established Geneva as a haven
  for the poor, persecuted, dispossessed and distressed.

- George Whitefield (1714-1770) began the first orphanage
  in Georgia.

- Charles Spurgeon (1834-1892) founded over 60 different charitable ministries.

- D. L. Moody (1837-1899) started over 150 street missions, soup kitchens, clinics, and rescue outreaches.[9]

This list could go on and on. True love has always shown itself in practical concern for all of the needs and problems of people. This has always been the true calling of evangelism and missions. No one says it better than George Grant in his excellent book entitled *In the Shadow of Plenty*:

When a missionary goes to a new mission field, what is the first thing he must do? His objective, of course, is to win souls, to make known the "peace" of Jesus Christ, but first he must win the right to be heard. He must exercise charity! He provides the people with medical care, food, shelter, clothing, pure water sources, proper sanitation and hygiene. He wins the confidence of his hearers and thus wins a hearing. . . . So charity is evangelism. It is discipleship. Or at the least it is the foundation for these tasks. Charity does not replace preaching, teaching or witnessing; instead it lays the groundwork. . . . Charity tills the soil so that it will be ready for . . . the seeds of salvation."[10]

A few years ago a friend of mine named Ray MacAnanny, a car dealer in Silver Spring, Maryland, set out to help some of the street people of Washington, D.C. In conjunction with a local church, he developed a morning breakfast for 250 people, started a discipleship program, and helped find jobs for many. Every morning he drove into Washington to flip pancakes, set up chairs, and serve "his men." One night he even arranged for a steak banquet for the street people complete with evening attire and presents! Nothing was asked in return. Ray soon became one of the most respected men in the city.

Involvement in charity brings leadership and allegiance. Human governments figured out long ago that the source of charity is also the source of power. He who provides is he who will be followed.

Most modern governments have endeavored to gain the allegiance of people through being the perceived rescuer from human suffering. Yet it is individuals and the Church of Jesus Christ who do the best job of meeting the needs of the poor and oppressed—if we understand that this is our role and do it. Whoever *does* understand and reaches out to serve the needy will be respected and will lead nations. As Christians wake up to this awesome responsibility and opportunity, we will get to know God as never before.

Spread Knowledge (Teaching)

Another key ingredient in good leadership is the communicating of knowledge. The Bible tells us that knowledge is power (Prov. 8:14). Leadership comes through the proper use of knowledge and understanding. This has a number of important aspects.

First, there is authority latent in knowledge itself. God created the Universe by the "spoken word." Through knowledge (the Bible uses the term *wisdom*), the heavens and earth were made (Prov. 8). Out of nothing, God spoke into existence all of the cosmos. Knowledge came out of the heart of the Creator, and the creation came into being as the effect.

In a limited sense, man has also experienced this power of the word. In the Bible, this is one reason why names and words were so important and sacred from the beginning. Words bring meaning. Words create realities in concert with God and His principles of communication. Ray Sutton explains:

> What is a name? A name in the Bible represents the person. The power to name is the power to control. God named Adam. Adam named the animals and Eve. This made man God's vice-regent in dominion. But the power to name is the power to have authority over the thing that is named. The Pharoah renamed Joseph (Gen. 41:45).

Nebuchadnezzar's official over the eunuchs renamed Daniel and the three Hebrew youths (Dan. 1:7). God renamed Abram to Abraham and Jacob to Israel, a sign of His authority over them.[11]

This power in naming, or using knowledge has been used through history to assert authority. When kingdoms were conquered the victors changed the names of the cities and states, bringing them under their domain.

In the political world, the power of words is an established fact. If one side can use its terms to frame a debate or issue, it has taken a long step down the road to acceptance and leadership. An example of this is the issue of abortion. After over 4,000 years of moral and verbal clarity, in the 1960s and 1970s a vocal minority in America convinced the public that a baby was a fetus—not a person, but simply a bundle of cells. Killing that baby inside her mother's womb became known as "terminating a pregnancy." As the language was changed, slowly the whole idea about what it meant to be a human being began to change. Leadership of an issue had been won through the power of words.

Knowledge is powerful stuff, and with proper motivation it can be used to greatly benefit people. In 1982, Jaime Escalante left a lucrative job in private industry to teach high school math in one of the worst areas of Los Angeles. His goal at Garfield High School was to give hope and self-esteem to poor Hispanic kids so that they could find meaningful jobs and become leaders in society.

Over much opposition, he started to teach calculus and win the confidence of his students. For weeks and months he taught them and pushed them in their capacities. When they were finally tested, all eighteen finished among the top two percent of students in America! In 1987, eighty-eight students from Garfield High completed the tests with honors. Many of these young people are now on their way to productive lives because of Jaime's leadership in imparting knowledge.

If Christians are to help guide the affairs of a nation, then truth via words must be used to reframe the issues and educate people. The battle for nations is ultimately a battle of words and ideas.[12] If we do not have better ideas, then we do not deserve to lead. This is especially true in the Information Age where knowledge and invention are increasing so rapidly.

This is why teaching and education are so vital to the individual Christian and the Church. Knowledge is power. The loving use of knowledge is wisdom. Churches that are relevant and make an impact on their area will be those who are training people to understand their world, minister to its needs, and change society through the conquering power of knowledge and love.

Be Devoted to Prayer

For we do not wrestle against flesh and blood, but against principalities, against powers, against the rulers of the darkness of this age, against spiritual hosts of wickedness in the heavenly places.

Therefore take up the full armor of God . . . praying always with all prayer and supplication in the Spirit (Eph. 6:12-18).

One of the easiest things to forget is that invisible spiritual warfare is taking place all around us daily. In Daniel 10 we see a vivid portrayal of this warfare in the heavenly realm. Daniel had been fasting and seeking God for three weeks. At the end of that time the angel Gabriel came to him with a message from God. He said "Do not fear, Daniel, for from the first day that you set your heart to understand, and to humble yourself before God, your words were heard; and I have come because of your words. But the prince of the kingdom of Persia withstood me twenty-one days; and behold, Michael, one of the chief princes came to help me. . . ." After revealing more details to this startled human being, the angel went on to say, "And now I must return to fight against the prince of Persia, and when I have gone forth, indeed the prince of Greece will come." (Dan. 10:10-21). He finished his message and was gone.

What a scene! While Daniel was praying for 21 days, a battle was going on in the heavenlies. Unseen beings had been in combat. A desperate war in the spirit realm had been raging. And Daniel had been involved. He had been in prayer. Somehow prayer had been used as a weapon in the invisible world. Due to Daniel's faithfulness and persistence, this battle was won for righteousness.

We may not consider ourselves Daniels or be graced with an angelic visitation in our lives, but the Bible teaches that each one of us is surrounded by this type of warfare every day. The people we face, the attitudes that confront us, the grit and grime of human affairs are not the real enemies. We do not battle primarily against human beings. Behind the human drama a cosmic war is going on between angels and demons in a breathtaking struggle for the souls of men. How much we need to remember this! How deeply we need to exercise authority and action in the place of prayer.

Prayer truly is the greatest source of power and authority on earth. Many times I have walked the corridors of Capitol Hill in Washington, D.C., watching the drama of American politics. I have observed as sides formed, heard the rhetoric, seen the human passions and struggle that shape issues and events. I have sat in the gallery of the Capitol Building watching intently as an important vote was cast. And many times I have asked the question: If my eyes were opened, what would I *really* see in the atmosphere all around me? Is the reality just the human personalities, fighting for their bill or project? In my heart, I know the answer was no. And so I have prayed, and exercised spiritual authority in situations. It *is* the greatest power. We must not forget.

Prayer is the greatest activity of a leader because it is the mark of his humility and the source of his greatest power. To pray is to acknowledge our need for God. To pray is to release the power of God into human affairs. It allows us, as Loren Cunningham says, to *create with God*. And the man or woman who prays shows a special understanding of the real world. It shows that he or she understands life is not just made up of men. Life is primarily a battle with an unseen enemy tugging at the hearts of men. Our greatest authority comes when we enter that battle through prayer.

A righteous leader who has authority on earth will first have authority in the heavenly realm. He will be a man of prayer. He will recognize that his true spirituality is in proportion to the maturity of his life in prayer. As Robert Murray McCheyne used to say so accurately, "What a man is on his knees before God, that's what he is—nothing more."

Exercise righteous leadership. Be a Daniel. Move in authority in the place of prayer and spiritual warfare.

Share the Gospel (Evangelism)

Another key to effective leadership is the important activity of evangelism. The heart of the Christian Gospel is that Jesus Christ came to earth to provide a way for men to be forgiven and restored to relationship to God. This is the Good News. Since His death and resurrection, this has been the central call of His Body, the Church. She is to proclaim to the world a message of hope and reconciliation.

The struggle for leadership on earth begins in the individual hearts of men. No matter how much we emphasize groups and nations, it is ultimately *individuals* that must make a decision to be restored to friendship with the living God. Our job as Christians is to give them that opportunity. This means that all of us must be involved in sharing our faith.

As Nate Krupp points out, the Early Church turned their world upside down because of their commitment to evangelism:

- Love was their motive (II Cor. 5:14);

- They meant business (Acts 4:20);

- They began where they were — Jerusalem (Luke 24:47);

- Everybody was involved (Mark 16:15);

- They did it everywhere they went (Mark 16:20);

- It was a natural activity (Acts 5:42, John 4);

- They were trained on the job (Acts 20:4);

- They were led by the Holy Spirit (Luke 24:49);

- They went in Jesus' authority (Acts 3:6, 16);

- They cared for their converts (Acts 15:36);

- They multiplied (II Tim. 2:2).[13]

Though the majority of the world may never become Christian, we must never forget that second to worship the single most important activity of the Kingdom of God is to bring in new subjects. This happens through a number of means, but the verbal communication of the Good News about Jesus Christ is basic. This will take great time and effort, but it is of extreme importance. Ray Sutton shares:

> God told the Israelites that their biblical culture would come "little by little." It did not come suddenly or overnight. . . . It can only successfully come about (and stick), if it takes hold at a grass roots level through evangelism. The expansion of the Gospel from Jerusalem to Rome serves as an example. It began in Jerusalem, and ended up in Rome. . . . The instrument the Holy Spirit used was evangelism.[14]

What is a major mark of the leadership of Billy Graham, or Loren Cunningham of Youth With A Mission, or Bill Bright of Campus Crusade For Christ? Is it not their consuming commitment to see all of the world evangelized? Through their influence they have drawn thousands of people into evangelism.

A righteous leader must be committed to evangelism. By this, he exercises authority in the spiritual world by helping to draw people "out of the domain of darkness and into the Kingdom of light." To lead peoples or nations, he must be able to lead individual souls. Leading them personally to Jesus Christ is a healthy and vitally necessary step.

Grow through Suffering

Some might find it curious to describe suffering as an action of leadership. Yet most leaders know it to be true. One who aspires to lead had better be prepared to walk a lonely road that includes many degrees and varieties of suffering. I am not referring here to wearing a martyr's cloak. Rather, it is a fact that those who walk out front in authority will face great difficulties and trials. If they are mature, they will learn from suffering some of the greatest lessons of leadership.

The greatest suffering was used to perfect the life of the world's greatest leader, Jesus Christ. As the writer to the Hebrews tells us:

> For it was fitting for Him, for whom are all things and by whom are all things, in bringing many sons to glory, to make the author of their salvation perfect through sufferings (Heb. 2:10).

Jesus was known as a "man of sorrows, acquainted with grief" (Isa. 53:3). He wept over the people. He battled the forces of darkness. His leadership ultimately took Him to death in shame, ridicule, and apparent defeat.

But suffering was the tool of deliverance that He used to set the world free from the clutches of sin. Christ's suffering disarmed his enemy. Difficulty proved the righteousness of His character. Suffering erased the final arguments as to what was truth and error. It was in His sufferings that the greatness of the true Messiah was seen.

Suffering follows leadership as the necessary price of its position. Those out front will make decisions not readily understood. They will be criticized, maybe laughed at, even ridiculed. Leaders will also be lonely, greatly pressured, and pulled in many directions.

All of this is not bad or wrong. If they are righteous leaders the rightness of their cause will only be demonstrated on the anvil of suffering. If they have godly authority, rejection and trial will only strengthen their character—and subsequent authority.

David is a case in point. In Gene Edwards' gripping dramatization, *A Tale of Three Kings*, he graphically describes how God shaped a shepherd boy into a leader in the "school of brokenness." For years David was hunted like a dog by the mad King Saul. God made David the "man after His own heart" through the tool of suffering. At one point in his life David completely gave up. At another, he pretended to be crazy. But through it all he was being built into a mighty man of God who would rule in humility and true authority.

To be a leader is to enroll in the school of trial and suffering. In that necessary activity, both we and our causes will be seen for what they really are. Suffering will test us. Suffering will prove us. Suffering will ultimately confirm us in the ways of righteous leadership.

Act as a Steward

Just as *servanthood* describes the overall attitude of leadership, *stewardship* encompasses the actions of the effective leader.

Man's original responsibility was to be a steward. The mandate given to man in the Garden of Eden was to cultivate and defend the creation of God. As a finite being, a miniature representation of an infinite God, man was placed on earth to take care of the grandeur that stretched before him. He was to name the animals and oversee them. He was to tend the ground. He was to multiply and fill the earth with myriads of descendants. His basic responsibility was to care for and wisely develop the resources of His Master.

Sin changed all that—and one of the greatest things that died was the concept of godly stewardship. Instead of tending, man neglected; instead of developing, he exploited; instead of enriching, he destroyed; instead of expanding the glories of life, he brought death and misery.

What is good stewardship? In Matthew 25:14-30, Jesus told about an owner giving various talents to his workers, and how he expected them to be good stewards of his resources. Two were wise stewards and were commended by their master. The third one neglected the wealth with which he was entrusted and received a great condemnation.

Philip Greenslade gives an excellent synopsis of stewardship in his book *Servant Leadership*:

- A steward is a man on trust

- A steward is given ability

- A steward is given responsibility

- A steward is accountable[15]

First, he states, a steward is a man on trust. He has been entrusted with the resources of others. He is given freedom by the Benefactor to exercise that trust. God gave enormous trust when He delegated the resources of the earth to us. Good, caring leadership will never abuse and exploit the earth's resources. Christian leaders should be the most concerned about the environment, ecology, and all aspects of creation. We have been given a trust: the earth.

Second, a righteous steward is given ability. God made man in His image, with awesome abilities of mind, will, and emotion. All the wonderful traits of personality and humanness were designed to be utilized in caring for creation.

Third, a steward is given responsibility. He is to use the resources he's been given responsibility over to fulfill a certain goal. That goal is to tend, develop, and rule in all aspects and cultural diversities for the glory and pleasure of God. The godly leader will see his task as the full development of all the earth under the lordship of Jesus Christ. He will apply this understanding to his business, family, relationships, hobbies—all aspects of life. In short, he will live out the principle that "whatever you do, do all to the glory of God" (I Cor. 10:31).

And finally, a steward is accountable to God and to others. He does not operate in a void. With the fear of God upon him, he tends to his responsibilities as a man who knows that a day of reckoning will come. There is no room for slovenliness. He cannot afford to be careless. A righteous leader will keep his conscience awake to be faithful to those he serves, and ultimately to his Maker. He is honest and transparent. Nothing can be hidden, so nothing *will* be hidden. With that awesome sense of stewardship, he serves his people well.

Graham Kerr, once known to millions on television as the Galloping Gourmet, gave his life to Christ in the 1970s after many years in a hollow Hollywood lifestyle of drinking, drugs, and an almost-ruined marriage. God put in the heart of Graham and his wife Treena a desire to use their skills in food and nutrition to help people around the world. They sent teams to Third World nations to teach agricultural methods. In the Western world, they encouraged believers to be better stewards in order to give to those in need. Many lives have been changed through the efforts of their stewardship.

The godly quality of stewardship sums up the actions of the one who walks in righteousness. He learns by the help and grace of God to manage well all the dimensions that are entrusted to him.

A New Type of Leader

The principles that we have mentioned in Chapters Four and Five are the keys to the future for the Body of Christ. Ultimately, all leadership boils down to the character of the leader. True authority comes from righteous behavior. Right living takes authority over evil in all dimensions and ways. This may not be seen immediately, but it eventually proves itself to be true.

Righteous attitudes and righteous actions—true leadership contains them both. For a number of years I have noticed that the liberal-left in America seem to project a greater measure of the righteous attitudes: a desire for justice, compassion for the needy, a cry for freedom and equality. On the other hand, the conservative-right seems to have greater understanding of the value of hard work, principles of knowledge, and other aspects of personal responsibility. Who is right? What is the Christian response?

Both are right, and the uniquely Christian response is the practice of them all. Compassionate attitudes with unwise actions will lead to failure (liberal politics). Knowledgeable actions with insensitive, uncaring hearts will leave the people cold (conservative politics).

The world is ripe for leadership that demonstrates a full slate of right attitudes and actions. This is not easy to do, but if anyone is capable of living it out, the followers of Christ must be. With His help and guidance we can be the servants and stewards for which the people of the earth are looking. The only question is, will we love God and people enough to serve in this way?

Do you want to be a leader? Are you already leading in various areas? Do you long for the Church to be a greater influence in the practical areas of life?

Then set your heart to be a righteous man or woman. Hunger and thirst for righteousness and you will be filled. Seek first the Kingdom of God and His righteousness and all that you need will be added unto you.

Learn to be a servant. Commit yourself to be a steward.

Be holy . . . . and live in obedience to God

Have faith . . . . and work His miracles

Live in hope . . . . and use your personal gifts

Walk in love . . . . and work harder than the rest

Have compassion . . . . and live a life of charity

Be committed to justice . . . and lead through knowledge

Be humble . . . . and do warfare in prayer

Be a unifier . . . . and proclaim the Good News

Make sacrifices . . . . and grow through suffering

Be a servant . . . . and act as God's steward

The Apostle Paul said in I Corinthians 4:1, "Let a man regard us in this manner, as servants of Christ and stewards of the mysteries of God." (NASB) The principles of the Kingdom are servanthood and stewardship. Let's emphasize them and God will give us authority among men.

For Thought and Application

1. What are the ten actions of good leadership? Why is the quality of stewardship a good description of them all?

2. Which of the ten are your strongest areas? In which of them are you weak? On which one should you concentrate in the next few weeks?

3. Should all civic leaders be measured by these qualities? How do the ones now running for office measure up? What should you do in light of this?

4. Do a thorough study of the one righteous action that interests you most. Apply your findings in your daily life.

PART TWO

THE CHALLENGE
OF LEADERSHIP

God is present in all life with the influence of His omnipresent and almighty power, and no sphere of human life is conceivable in which religion does not maintain its demands, that God shall be praised, that God's ordinances shall be observed, and that every labor shall be permeated with fervent and ceaseless prayer.

Wherever man may stand, whatever he may do, to whatever he may apply his hand in agriculture, commerce or industry, or his mind in the world of art and science, he is, in whatsoever it may be, constantly standing before the face of his God.[1]

Abraham Kuyper

SIX

CHANGING A NATION

In the summer of 1975, Loren Cunningham, the founder of Youth With A Mission, was spending some time with his family in a cabin in Colorado. He used the days to seek God and pray for future direction.

One day in prayer, he was impressed with some influential areas that Christians should target to turn around nations for God. He grabbed a pen and paper and scribbled them down:

1. The home

2. The Church

3. The government

4. The schools

5. Arts and entertainment

6. The media

Loren put the piece of paper in his pocket.

Later that week, Loren and his wife, Darlene, met with Bill and Vonette Bright, the leaders of Campus Crusade for Christ. As they shared in a time of fellowship, Bill said, "Loren, God has shown me several ways to change a nation." He then began to share what God had laid upon his heart. Dumbfounded, Loren listened as Bill related them— areas of society that influenced the life of a country. Written on the folded sheet of paper in Loren's pocket were the same concepts that God had shown to him! After Bill finished, he pulled out the paper and they shook their heads in amazement. Except for the occasional difference of synonyms, God had given these two spiritual leaders the *same list*!

The list has been refined somewhat since that summer. Loren believed he was to add "business" to the list of influence-makers. But what God was underscoring by giving this perspective to both Bill Bright and Loren Cunningham was an area of truth vital to our understanding of leadership. It is imperative that we understand the various realms of leadership that exist in human societies — *sphere sovereignty* — and how these different spheres operate independently and collectively.

Sphere Sovereignty

In Romans 13:1-2, Paul gives us the following perspective:

> Let every soul be subject to the governing authorities. For there is no authority except from God, and the authorities that exist are appointed by God. Therefore, whoever resists the authority resists the ordinance of God, and those who resist will bring judgment on themselves.

He then goes on to apply this to civil government, and gives us the purpose of governmental authority. Paul concludes with:

> Render, therefore, to all their due: Taxes to whom taxes are due, customs to whom customs, fear to whom fear, honor to whom honor (verse 7).

In this passage Paul illustrates that God has established many authorities, or spheres of leadership in the world. There is not *one* authority. There are many authorities. These have all been established by God, and are necessary for order and control. This text in Romans is specifically talking about one of the spheres of authority — civil governments. But there are others.

All through the Bible and in our everyday experience, we see the reality of multiple spheres of leadership. We see the supreme authority of God. We are told of the heavenly authority of the angels. We recognize the authority of the individual, in various talents, graces, and giftings. On earth we are well acquainted with parental authority; the authority of the Church; the various levels of civil government — from the local school board to the federal power. There are also the influential areas of society to which Bill Bright and Loren were alerted.

These spheres of authority are unique and independent, but they also blend together to form the tapestry of human culture. The sovereignty of God reigns above them all, yet to all of them we owe a specific honor, or *due*, as Paul said in Romans 13. To understand life clearly is to discern these spheres and their relationship to one another under God. If we relate to them and live within them according to God's design, they become the supports of order, freedom and blessing.

Guillaume Groen van Prinsterer of the Netherlands, a devout Christian thinker and politician in the early to midnineteenth century, was the first to use the phrase *souvereiniteit in eigen sfeer* — sovereignty within its own sphere — with respect to the multiple authorities of life.[2] Van Prinsterer began a political movement in Holland called the Anti-Revolutionaries (or Christian Historicals) which began to live out his principles of drawing a clear distinction between God-given spheres of government and the Church. He had a great burden for education and held high posts in government. However, during his lifetime he was basically a general without an army, and it was left to a spiritual and ideological protégé to fully develop the concept.[3]

That successor was Abraham Kuyper (1837-1920), whom we noted in Chapter Two. Kuyper was not only a great thinker, but a statesman (serving in Parliament for a number of years, and Prime Minister of the Netherlands from 1901-1905); a journalist (editor of the daily newspaper *De Standaard* for over 40 years); an educator (he founded the Free University in Amsterdam in 1880; a pastor, theologian, and reformer in the Dutch Reformed Church; and a prolific author of books spanning fifty years.[4]

Obviously Kuyper was a giant of a man. Through his indefatigable efforts over fifty years of public life, the subsequent history of the Netherlands was greatly improved. What was his guiding motivation? In his own words:

> One desire has been the ruling passion of my life. . . . That in spite of all worldly opposition, God's holy ordinances shall be established again in the home, in the school, and in the State for the good of the people; to carve as it were into the conscience of the nation the ordinances of the Lord . . . until the nation pays homage again to God.[5]

Kuyper believed that all of life was under the authority of God and the lordship of Jesus Christ. He believed that Christ came to earth to redeem all aspects of the Fall, including human society and culture. He said:

> I discovered that the Holy Scripture does not only cause us to find justification by faith, but also discloses the foundation of all human life, the holy ordinances which must govern all human existence in Society and State.[6]

It was Abraham Kuyper who expanded the concept of "sovereignty in the individual social spheres," which he divided into seven areas—family, religion (the Church), the state (civil governments), education, business vocation, the arts, and science. He then divided these seven areas into two different spheres. He comments:

> The sovereignty of God, in its descent upon men, separates itself into two spheres. On the one hand, the mechanical sphere of State authority, and on the other hand the organic sphere of the authority of the social circles. And in both these spheres the inherent authority is sovereign, that is to say, it has above itself nothing but God.[7]

In all these spheres . . . State government cannot impose its laws, but must reverence the innate laws of life. God rules in these spheres, just as supremely and sovereignly through His chosen virtuosi, as He exercises dominion in the sphere of the State itself, through His chosen magistrates.[8]

The concept of sphere authority was foundational to Kuyper's world view. God was the Supreme Sovereign, with all other authority delegated by Him. On earth were various jurisdictions, all responsible directly to God and designed to operate independently and in complementary unity. The state, or civil government, was a sphere where officials were to operate according to God's ordinances (Rom. 13). But there were other spheres that were to be completely independent of state authority, but also directly accountable to God. These were the various "social circles," like family, Church, education, and arts.

Kuyper lived a tireless and productive life, applying this vital biblical truth in many arenas. He had grasped a powerful key to unlock the understanding of the various authorities of life. He laid a foundation for a biblical understanding of leadership and authority—and how one goes about actually changing a nation.

I would like to concentrate on seven primary spheres of influence within a nation or culture. It is in these domains that the day-to-day challenge of leadership takes place. It is here that God's sovereignty, angelic influence, and man's autonomy are all brought into action and form.

The Family

The basic unit of any society is the family. It is the first sphere of authority we encounter as we enter the world. Even if we are orphans, someone steps in to fulfill this function. Throughout most of our lives, the family is a primary molder of our character and values. After the sovereignty of the individual under God, it is the most important sphere of nurture and guidance that helps us become who we are.

The family is clearly ordained by God. It was God who created the first people, and who formed them into a family (Gen. 2:18-25). It was God who blessed them with children and commanded them to be fruitful and multiply. The Bible teaches that every family in heaven and on earth derives its very name from God (Eph. 3:15).

Though various cultures have different expressions and configurations of the family unit, all cultures have families as the heart and core of society. Nations are basically associations of families. This is also the essence of tribal life. But the foundational unit is a father and mother, their children, and sometimes grandparents and other extended relatives.

The family is one of three God-ordained institutions (the other two being the Church and civil government). The family has been given the right to impose a binding promise upon husband and wife. This oath—to remain committed to one another for life—is taken during the wedding ceremony and symbolized by the wedding ring. It is a vow made to God and not to men. The family also has another symbol of authority: the rod, to be used for discipline and correction. All this authority is God-given, and the Bible is replete with God's standards for family life.

A primary responsibility of the family is education (Prov. 22:6, Deut. 11:18,19). God has given parents the responsibility to give training in values, character, knowledge, and life-experience. In modern life, this concept has nearly disappeared and been relegated by default to state-supported schools. This was never God's intention, and has resulted in a form of state tyranny over the family. Now two different spheres are battling for the hearts and minds of the young generation.

The Western world has also experienced a demise of the family that threatens its very future. Allan Bloom comments on this sad state of the American family:

> The loss of the gripping inner life . . . must be primarily attributed not to our schools or political life, but to the fam-

ily. . . . The dreariness of the family's spiritual landscape passes belief. It is as monochrome and unrelated to those who pass through it as are the barren steppes frequented by nomads who take their mere subsistence and move on. The delicate fabric of the civilization into which the successive generations are woven has unraveled, and the children are raised, not educated. [Parents] have nothing to give their children in the way of a vision of the world. Fathers and mothers have lost the idea that the highest aspiration they might have for their children is for them to be wise.[9]

As the family goes, so goes the nation. If you want to give leadership to a nation, you must strengthen its families. If you want to destroy a society, the surest way is to break down the strength and righteousness of the family.

My wife and I have four children within four and a half years of age. Our first son, Nathan, was born after God gave us a promise while ministering in the Soviet Union. His word to us was "at this time next year you will bear a son." A year to the week later our child of promise came.

Two years later our twins, David and Bethany, were born on Father's Day. What a present that was for me! The only downside was that for a few months we had three children in diapers and I had one tired wife! Two and one half years later our little Megan was born. All four of our children were born on Sunday.

Our family is one of our richest treasures. They are our greatest joy, and also our deepest challenge. They produce our lowest moments of failure and struggle and our greatest feelings of blessing and accomplishment. Nurturing our family in the ways of God is one of our highest callings. We want to raise nation-changers that can, should the Lord tarry, help rebuild our society.

The family is a God-ordained sphere of authority. Parents are responsible to God for their children's livelihood and their future.[10] No societal domain is more important. None can experience the heights of joy and fruitfulness, or fathom the depths of sorrow and dissolution as the family can.

The Church

A second God-ordained sphere on earth is the Church. In Matthew 16:18, 19, nearly two thousand years ago, Jesus boldly proclaimed to Simon Peter:

> On this rock I will build My Church, and the gates of Hades shall not prevail against it. And I will give you the keys of the kingdom of heaven, and whatever you bind on earth will be bound in heaven, and whatever you loose on earth will be loosed in heaven.

God intended the Church to have clear leadership on the earth. First, let's understand what we mean by the Church. What we do *not* mean is some ecclesiastical structure or denomination. Jesus did not come to build a new bureaucracy — He came to call people to Himself. Those "called out ones" (in the Greek, *ekklesia*), both in heaven and on earth are the Church. The Church is redeemed people — in all walks of life, and in all denominations and groups. This is the meaning of the word in the Bible.

God has given the Church some vital responsibilities to fulfill. One is to lead individuals to a saving knowledge of Christ. Only those who know the living God can lead others into that same knowledge. You can only reproduce what you are. The people of God possess the unique capacity to stimulate and nurture discipleship. This is where the real life of the corporate Church should be in operation — in teaching, fellowship, the breaking of bread, and prayer (Acts 2:42). The Church brings new believers to birth, and the Church also has a fundamental role in the growth of its children toward spiritual adulthood.

The Body of Christ and its many expressions also have a basic responsibility toward the poor and needy. It is almost a foreign concept to us in an era of big government and institutionalized welfare, but God intended the Church to be the primary agency of compassion and welfare. This was true in the Old Testament via the Levitical function, and was clearly established in the New Testament Church. Caring people are those who serve the needy best. Many studies have shown that state-run welfare programs have been an abysmal failure.[11] Senator Mark Hatfield has pointed out that if every church and synagogue took care of only ten poor families, poverty would be totally eliminated in America. Instead we spend billions of dollars a year through impersonal agencies and the number of those who live in poverty only increases.

But the fault is not civil government's: The government has only taken over welfare because the twentieth century Church has abdicated her responsibility. The government was never designed to meet people's needs. That is outside its God-given sphere of leadership. That role was given to the Church. We need to repent of this failing.

The Church has also been given the central role of prophetically proclaiming God's moral standards. Relationally, the Church is the family of God. In terms of its mission and function, the Church is the agency that extends the Kingdom of God in the earth. The business of the Church is the Kingdom of God. The Church is also the "pillar and ground of the truth" (I Tim. 3:15). With Jesus as the Head, the Body of Christ is on earth to announce His lordship and to be a beacon of truth for every other area of life and sovereignty.

In the Bible, the Church of Jesus Christ is likened to both salt and light in the midst of a tasteless and darkened world. The Church has the power to demonstrate righteousness to a world that has no moral coordinates. Light always exposes and conquers darkness. Salt always enriches that which is bland. The true power to change things lies in the realm of the saints. That's why Jesus said:

> You are the salt of the earth; but if the salt loses its flavor, how shall it be seasoned? It is then good for nothing but to be thrown out and trampled under foot by men. You are the light of the world. A city that is set on a hill cannot be hidden. Nor do they light a lamp and put it under a basket,

but on a lampstand, and it gives light to all who are in the
house. Let your light so shine before men that they may
see your good works and glorify your Father in heaven
(Matt. 5:13-16).

The Church was established by Jesus Christ to shine the
light of His salvation into all aspects and dimensions of life
upon this globe.

As a sphere of influence, the Church has no equal. The
reason is simple: Christ dwells in His fullness in the Church.
And He possesses all authority. When His people abide in
Him, they also possess all authority, that "the manifold wisdom of God might be made known by the Church to the
principalities and powers in the heavenly places" (Eph. 3:10).

The Church was meant to influence all other spheres,
but this does not mean that the Church can take authority
from other realms not given to her. The Church is not the
family, and the Church is not the state. But Christians are
called of God to shed the light of the Gospel into every area
of life through serving—and in her own sphere, to govern
her affairs well. The Church is truly the world's prophet of
truth and servant of mercy. If she does not shine in the darkness, the world will know no light.

Civil Government

The third God-ordained sphere of authority in society is
civil government (Rom. 13). Notice the term *civil* government. Why not the more commonly used term, *government*?
It is important to remember that there are many governments in the universe. God has a government. Angels have
a government. Man has individual, self-government. And
then there are civil governments ordained among men.
These *governments* (including school boards, county, city,
state and federal governments) are commanded by God to
be *civil*, or righteous (Rom. 13:4). So there are many layers
of civil governments on earth, each with its realm of juris-
diction. Why do they exist? Abraham Kuyper explains:

The principal characteristic of government is the right of life and death. According to the apostolic testimony the magistrate bears the sword, and this sword has a threefold meaning. It is the sword of justice, to mete out corporeal punishment to the criminal. It is the sword of war, to defend the honor and the rights and the interests of the State against its enemies. It is the sword of order, to thwart at home all forcible rebellion.[12]

Civil government has been established by God as His servant to maintain true freedom and orderly peace. This can only be done through exercising the power of the sword — sanctions — against those things that are wrong in society. Thus we have fines, jails, prisons, and capital punishment (for the worst of crimes — murder). This is necessary because man is fallen, and civil government is to protect men from the sins of other men. In an imperfect world, there has to be protection for the innocent. This is done through good laws and appropriate penalties.

John Brabner-Smith, a constitutional lawyer, points out that every country must have a "Purpose for Society" — a charter that is the *law above the law*. In the United States this is the Declaration of Independence. This charter must then have by-laws that conform to it (in the U.S. this document is the Constitution). Government is the agency which carries out the purpose of society according to the by-laws.

Laws are to be made by civil governments, and backed up by penalties, to serve God in the protection of people against the ravages of wrong behavior. Laws and government were designed to build walls holding back sin for the public good. Good civil governments serve God and bring freedom and orderly peace to people. As Mr. Kuyper said, the sword of government is a sword of justice, and it is also a sword of order. It becomes a bent and twisted sword when it does not operate by God's laws.

Many governments today no longer understand what they were ordained to do. They acknowledge no divine standard for establishing good laws. The leaders rarely, if ever, think of themselves as serving God. Frequently they don't serve the people either. You can't serve people properly unless you first serve God and follow His rules for behavior. Without this you are left to flounder in an ocean of public opinion, shifting values, and personal gain.

This is the Western dilemma. In rejecting God's laws as the basis for right and wrong, we are being smothered by the effects of unrestrained sin. People cheat on their taxes. The prisons are overflowing. Sexual liberation is destroying the family and has brought about the venereal disease plague, including AIDS. Crime is rampant, and politicians are confused. Why are we in this mess? Why is society breaking down?

It's simple. Civil government is not doing its God-ordained function. It is not creating true freedom and order in society by serving God, enacting His laws, and in so doing, serving people. The twentieth century is viewing a vivid lesson in the West, the Communist world, and also the Islamic states: Civil governments that do not function on God's principles hurt people and destroy cultures. It is happening all around us. The laws and philosophies of men have failed. The rubble is everywhere. As in all other areas of authority, the civil governments of our day need to be rebuilt and reformed to reflect God's intended standards and function.

What will that bring? Liberty and justice for all. That was the original intention. Civil governments were designed by God in a fallen cosmos to protect man from himself. In these areas of civil justice, only governments have the right to restrain and to punish.

The societal spheres of the family, the Church, and civil government are the three primary areas of influence that give leadership and order to society. Each is a distinct realm, and should not encroach on the God-ordained sphere of another. The family is foundational and the primary molder of character. The Church is both pastoral (caring for the needs of people) and prophetic (speaking God's truth into all arenas). Civil government is to protect these and the other spheres from the damaging effects of sin.

But there are four other spheres in human society that exercise leadership. They may not have the right to binding oaths or penal sanctions, but as God-given "domains" they exercise great influence in the shaping and maintaining of human culture.

Education

A tremendous area of influence in any human society is the area of education. Knowledge is power. Education brings authority and influence. Those who control education in any nation or tribe will have great influence on the direction of that particular people.

That is why political revolutionaries have always sought to control education. They have recognized its latent power. When the Bolsheviks came to power in the Soviet Union one of the first things they did was take over the schools. All children had to go to school and what was taught was totally determined by the state. To have domination over the masses, the domain of education had to be controlled by the government. They recognized the authority of the sphere of education and seized it.

Likewise in all history, major battles were fought for leadership of the sphere of education. Martin Luther, in arguing for the Bible to be foundational to education, said strongly:

I am much afraid that schools will prove to be wide gates to hell unless they diligently labor in explaining the Holy Scriptures, engraving them in the hearts of youth. I advise no one to place his child where the Scriptures do not reign paramount. Every institution in which men are not constantly occupied with the Word of God must become corrupt.

When education becomes corrupt, people become corrupt. When education is godly, righteous people are produced. What and how children are taught greatly affect the direction of a whole civilization.

Whose responsibility is it to educate children? Is it the state's or the Church's? And what kind of education does God require it to be?

Let's allow the Bible to speak for itself:

> Hear, O Israel: The Lord our God, the Lord is one! You shall love the Lord your God with all your heart, with all your soul, and with all your might. And these words which I command you today shall be in your heart; you shall teach them diligently to your children, and shall talk of them when you sit in your house, when you walk by the way, when you lie down, and when you rise up (Deut. 6:4-7).

The words couldn't be clearer: Education must be centered around God and His truth. And it is the family — parents — that are given the authority from God to educate their children. Bob Thoburn, a long-time Christian educator in the state of Virginia explains:

> All the books on education ever written in the history of the world are not worth what we learn from these four verses. All the lectures on education ever given in the most esteemed universities of the world cannot equal the wisdom they contain. The two principles are: 1. Education is to be God-centered. 2. Education is a parental responsibility.[13]

Children are born to parents, not to the state, not to the Church, nor to any other institution. God gives His authority to the family to educate the children — and that is to be done according to His character and ways. Parents can delegate that authority to another arena of government (thus we have government schools, parochial schools, Christian schools and the like). But the true authority lies with the parents. God holds them responsible for educating their children. Children are their trust. Christian education is their duty.

When parents assume their God-given responsibility to train up their children in the way they should go, they exercise true leadership in a realm that itself guides the culture. As we rapidly explore the deeper reaches of the Information Age, the sphere of education will loom greater and greater. In a world of accelerating information, education and the wisdom to use it rightly will play increasing roles. This is why Austin Kiplinger comments:

In 1925 Calvin Coolidge said, "The business of America is business." Today I say the business of America is *education*. Education constructs the foundations of technology, and technology in turn provides the track for industry and commerce to advance into the twenty-first century.

It is estimated that ninety percent of all scientific knowledge has been generated in the past three decades or so. Roughly the same proportion of all scientists and engineers in the world's history are now alive and working. It's probable that both their numbers *and* the base of scientific knowledge will double by [the year] 2000 around the world.[14]

The battle for the twenty-first century will greatly center around the field of education. Education will shape the future. It has authority. The question remains: Whose authority will it be? Will Christian parents in concert with the Church set the agenda, or will others lead our children into a very different future?

Business
(including Science and Technology)

Another sphere of great influence is business. This is man combining his knowledge and talents in the development of the physical creation. Its common name is *work*! We are including the areas of science and technology under this category because science is the discipline of knowledge of the created world, and the development of technology is related because it is most greatly applied to the realm of commerce. This particular sphere is the vocational domain of man and has a profound influence on the direction of culture and nations.

As in all realms of authority, the realm of business is God-ordained. Before man's fall in Eden, God gave Adam the job of tending the Garden (Gen. 2:15). Man's work was part of the original mandate to "subdue" the earth, and the fall didn't change that commandment—it only made its realization more difficult. God said, "in toil you shall eat of it" and "in the sweat of your face you shall eat bread" (Gen. 3:17, 19).

Man was born for labor and development. He was given a mind to search out the knowledge of the universe. He was given the physical strength and skill to harness its energies and resources. The major effect of the fall was to make work survival-oriented rather than the pure delight of development in paradise. But this curse was also a blessing: The realm of business or day-to-day work is one of the most creative areas of life as well as a great restraint on evil. The fact that men have to work for a living keeps them out of many aspects of sin. There is nothing worse than a depraved mind abusing the resources of paradise.

When Christ came to earth, His mission was to bring redemption to all aspects of the cosmos. His primary focus was man. But sin had caused the world to be affected, and the death of Jesus brought a liberating force to all of creation. As individuals became reconciled to God, their abilities could be harnessed to righteously bring changes and hope to the equally fallen environment. With the transformation of the human mind through Christ, a world view could be brought into effect that viewed the future with confident expectation, and the created order with purpose and meaning.

Thus it was Christianity that gave birth to modern science. An intelligent Being created an orderly universe and gave man the finite abilities to understand and "tend it." Through Christ, man's mind was set free to view the world in greater clarity—and it was out of this revelation that science as we know it, and the technological era came into being. The world's first great scientists, such as Galileo, Sir Isaac Newton, and later, Michael Faraday, were men with a Christian world view. Design pointed to a Designer, and it was the calling of man to explore that design and harness it for the glory of God and the good of mankind. Once again it is Abraham Kuyper who gives us the perspective:

> The object of the work of redemption is not limited to the salvation of individual sinners, but extends itself to the redemption of the world, and to the organic reunion of all things in heaven and on earth under Christ as their original head.

> Calvinism called Christendom back to the order of creation: "Replenish the earth, subdue it and have dominion over everything that lives upon it." Christian life as a pilgrimage was not changed, but the (Christian) became a pilgrim, who, while on his way to his eternal home, had yet to perform on earth an important task. The cosmos, in all the wealth of the kingdom of nature, was spread out before, under, and above man. This entire limitless field had to be worked. . . . And so it came to pass that the people itself, who had until now refrained from encouraging science, by a new and a sparkling energy, suddenly called it into action, spurring it on to a sense of liberty, hitherto entirely unknown.[15]

Physical work has great meaning and value. It is man combining his knowledge and talents with the physical creation—bringing it under his authority, and through Christ, causing it to be sanctified and redeemed. It is a job, but also a trust. God has given us the world to be worthy stewards over, and it is in the realm of business that we truly "get our hands dirty."

The domain of commerce (as enhanced and developed by science and technology) is a major area of leadership in the earth. Those who work hard in the service of God and others will reap His benefits both in this life and the next. One of the greatest ways to change a nation is to harness knowledge, talent, and physical resources in the commercial realm of life. Successful businessmen attain great power and influence in their communities and nations. They can use this wrongly for selfish profit and gain, or they can assume righteous leadership of immense proportions.

Labor, work, and business are the normal everyday world. It is also a primary sphere in which to exercise servant leadership. Most of us have to work. We can either be ruled by it, or take rulership over it. Those who do so for the glory of God will exercise great authority in the development of life and human culture in the nations of the earth. The Apostle Paul said, "Do your work heartily as for the Lord rather than for men; knowing that from the Lord you will receive the reward of the inheritance. It is the Lord Christ whom you serve" (Col. 3:23, 24 NASB).

The Arts
(including Entertainment and Sports)

Nobody doubts the power of the arts. Artistic forms are as diverse as mankind, yet they have major influence in everything we do. Art in all its forms is the language of the heart— the attempt by man to communicate the meaning of life and the "highs" and "lows" of human existence. Art is expression and communication, and thus art is power. In today's world, as always, its realm of authority is almost unrivaled—we flee to it for comfort, ecstasy, and meaning.

In a universe dimmed by the effects of sin, art allows us to drink from a higher fountain. This was true from the very beginning of man. Abraham Kuyper explains:

> Calvin esteemed art, in all its ramifications, as a gift from God, or, more especially, as a gift of the Holy Ghost; that he fully grasped the profound effects worked by art upon the life of the emotions; that he appreciated the end for which art had been given, viz., that by it we might glorify

God, and ennoble human life, and drink at the fountain
of higher pleasures, yea even of common sport; and finally, that so far from considering art as a mere imitation
of nature, he attributed to it the noble vocation of disclos-
ing to man a higher reality that was offered to us by this
sinful and corrupted world.[16]

The sphere of the arts is truly the domain of the soul. As
sin has scarred the beauty of life and blurred its source in
God, art has been His gift to man to elevate him back into
the divine presence. Art is the medium through which man
endeavors to make his way back into the glories of lost paradise. It is a mirror image of the joys and tragedies of the
human soul, searching for virtue and meaning, and longing
for a way to make the spiritual inhabit physical form.

In a world that has lost confidence in authoritative structures, the arts have risen higher and higher in influence. Because of the abuses of civil government, the deadness of the
organized Church, and the lack of intimacy in the family,
the twentieth century has seen a major flight of people into
the realm of the arts to give meaning to life. These include
some very contemporary and unusual forms:

Music: Who can doubt the power of music in our day?
The heroes of the past two generations have been the rock
stars. I remember seeing the Beatles in person in 1964 as an
eleven-year-old who was looking for excitement and meaning. They still wore green suits, and their hair was relatively
short. But thousands screamed and yelled and literally wor-
shipped the stage they walked on. In the ensuing years, they
and others led a whole generation into promiscuous sex,
drugs, eastern religions, and an entire cultural revolution.
From Elvis to Mick Jagger, from Prince to Michael Jackson,
the leaders of the 60s, 70s, and 80s have been *musical gurus*,
exercising a strange power over masses of people.

Music as an art form carries tremendous power and authority. Someone once said, "Allow me to write the ballads of
a nation and I care not who makes its laws." The library of
today's youth is a collection of record albums and disks.

Their symbol of devotion is the ever-present Walkman, worn like a modern helmet to protect and tantalize the brain.

Entertainment: From nightclubs to discos, from movie theaters to television, entertainment in the West has become one of its primary expressions of art. Though some would deny that these things are artistic expression, there is no denying the fact that they are sensual pursuits of meaning, and symbols of the values of contemporary culture. Modern man doesn't want to think. He wants to feel and be entertained. He doesn't believe greatly in the divine, so all that is left is the experience of the earthly. Today's heroes are entertainers and movie stars. Discos have become the "churches" of the youth, and prime-time television has replaced poetry, reading, and devotion. This, nonetheless, is art. And it is discipling a world in its ways and values.

Sports: This is another expression of art that has become big business in Western nations. Sports have become a search for excellence, a way of venting frustration, and a subliminal way to play out the conflict between good and evil (as expressed in two opposing teams). Going to the football game is better than the sensual expression of most church services: There is worship (cheering), fellowship (over peanuts and hot dogs), communion (beer drinking), and a complete service (the game). Sunday in America now contains a number of altars: Probably the most popular one has a remote control, color screen, and is attached to a VCR. And next to musicians and movie stars, athletes are the heroes of the young. They do the modern day "paintings"—in Dolby stereo and living Technicolor.

Mentioning these modern art forms is not meant to downplay the power and beauty of the more traditional fine arts. These still have tremendous influence. But I have highlighted the above because they have captured the attention of the twentieth century masses. Leadership has been exercised and millions of people are following contemporary Pied Pipers. Art in all its forms has great power and authority. The only question is: Who will be the artists, and what kind of message and values will they encourage humanity to follow?

The Media

The media is a major sphere of authority in most areas of the modern world. Since the invention of the printing press, the media has increased in influence decade after decade. Today in American politics, it is a foregone conclusion that the use of television and other media forms is a major factor in who becomes President of the United States or who occupies the halls of Congress.

The media is a multiplier of knowledge. Power and authority lie in having information, but the people who determine *what* information is to be shared and *how* it is shared have truly become the power brokers. With the advent of radio and television in this century, the media has begun to exercise almost a global monopoly on history and perceived reality. Whoever does the reporting is the one who writes history.

Let me give an example. The 1980 Washington For Jesus rally drew hundreds of thousands to the U.S. capital for a day of prayer and national repentance. During the day we spoke with the Washington Park Police who were doing the official estimate of the crowd, which they eventually posted as 650,000 attendees. We asked one of them if there had ever been a larger gathering in Washington, D.C. He replied, "Yes, there was one gathering in the early 70s of about 800,000 people—but it was never reported." "Never reported?" we responded. "Why not?" The official replied, "Well, the event was unpopular with the media at that time, and so they reported the crowd at only 200,000."

That evening the papers came out on our Christian event. The estimate of the crowd in the papers was 200,000! In one newspaper, this gathering of over half a million people was relegated to an inside page, and a story about 10 people involved in a sit-in at National Airport was given a prominent headline! Talk about writing history. Ten people at an airport demonstration was greater news than 650,000 who had come from all fifty states and many nations to pray for America!

During the last century, before the age of electronic
media, the American revivalist, Charles Finney, said there
were two primary reasons for the decay of conscience that
was taking place in America. This was his assessment:

> I believe it is a fact generally admitted that there is much
> less conscience manifested by men and women in nearly
> all walks of life than there was forty years ago. There is
> justly much complaint of this, and there seems to be little
> prospect of reformation. The rings and frauds and villain-
> ies in high and low places, among all ranks of men, are
> most alarming, and one is almost compelled to ask: "Can
> anybody be safely trusted?" Now what is the cause of this
> degeneracy? Doubtless there are many causes that con-
> tribute more or less directly to it, but I am persuaded that
> the fault is more in the ministry and the public press than
> in any and all things else.[17]

Finney believed that the ministers of the Church were
primarily to blame for declining morals. They should have
been shining the light of the Gospel into the nation. But
secondarily, he believed the media was to blame. It was beginning to publish much "darkness," and blindness of conscience was the result.

I wonder what Mr. Finney would say about the power of
the media in this century? With dial-a-porn, X-rated cable
television, and sexually-oriented network TV, all intruding
into the homes of America, he would certainly be shocked.
What was happening in his day was miniscule compared to
the power of today's media to influence the hearts and minds
of people.

Not all the media in our day are bad, of course. There
are many excellent newsmen who try to be fair in their
reporting. There is also the advent of large-scale Christian
radio, television, and print ministries. Yet according to a
Columbia University study done in 1982, the media in the
United States are far more anti-religious and far more liberal in their political views than the average American. This

means we are being given a definite slant on current events. On one occasion President Reagan quipped, "You fellows do more writing of the news than actually reporting it."

All forms of communication media have tremendous power and authority. In some ways it has even altered the American concept of justice. For many years a person accused of a crime was considered innocent until proven guilty. Today once a name is accused in print the person is assumed to be guilty until proven innocent. Ray Donovan, a former secretary of labor under President Reagan, was acquitted of fraud charges. He remarked, "Now where do I go to get back my reputation?" The press had branded him. It was almost impossible for him to regain his good name.

The media is a sphere of authority that has become very powerful in the world. What it is like is determined by those who control it. No matter who they are, their authority will continue to be great.

Molding the Fabric of a Nation

The seven societal spheres of authority that we have briefly sketched . . .

- the family
- the Church
- civil government
- education
- business
- the arts
- and the media . . .

are the spheres of power that give leadership and direction to a city, state, province, or nation. God is the supreme authority, and is author and delegator of all other realms. On earth he has given to men various institutions or power structures through which authority and influence flow. All of these categories must be subject to His laws and principles. All are important.

Each of these spheres has power to mold the thoughts and hearts of people on the earth. But each must submit itself to its God-given domain. Whenever any sphere takes on authority not given to it by God, the result is despotism. When the Church infringes on the God-given authority of the state, that is tyranny. When the state attempts to take from the family the God-given responsibility of education, that is tyranny. When the media tries to be the conscience of the nation over that of the Church, that is tyranny. When the arts are used to encourage rebellion against the just laws of the state, that is tyranny. When business tries to put down the God-given rights of the individual worker, that is tyranny.

The spheres can only produce liberty and justice when they operate according to divine balance and design. None of them are God. None of them have supreme authority over another. All have been given by God to perpetuate order and happiness in a fallen world. They are God's form of checks and balances in a world where men so easily abuse one another.

Whether these spheres will operate in balance has always been a key question. This can only happen if Christians understand their importance, and do everything in their power to influence and give leadership to them.

Someone, or some group, will always assume leadership in these society-shaping areas. Satan is aware of that, and has ordered his evil empire to capture these principalities. In actuality, this is a primary way that Satan controls the earth. He has a limited number of fallen angels. The population of the earth continues to grow into the billions. As the population of the earth grows, his strategy is to capture the power structures.

The Marxists have understood the power of the sphere areas in their violent revolutions. They have never needed a majority — just a committed minority who will make necessary sacrifices to take over government structures, education, the press, the arts, and to nationalize industry. In the Soviet Union, a small group of people control a nation of over 250 million because they have captured the authority structures of the country. When you're the minority and moving in unrighteous forms of leadership, you have to "go for the jugular" to have any hope of victory.

This has astounding implications for Christians today. With humanism failing, and the developing nations looking for a model to follow, the Church is being given an opportunity to build and rebuild the nations of the earth. To do this, we need to understand *how* authority flows through God-given spheres of influence. And we need to understand how to turn a nation around.

We will do this as we begin to exercise righteous, servant leadership in all these various spheres. We must not seek to control, but truly seek to serve. We can't act from a heart of manipulation, but must seek to apply God's wisdom to all domains of power.

But first we need to be convinced that Jesus Christ came to bring redemption and deliverance to all dimensions of life. We begin with our world view. We have to perceive that true Christianity was designed to enlighten and change the entire world. In the words of Abraham Kuyper:

[Christianity] has wrought an entire change in the world of thoughts and conceptions . . . it has not only honored man for the sake of his likeness to the Divine image, but also the world as a Divine creation. . . . Thus domestic life regained its independence, trade and commerce realized their strength in liberty, art and science were set free . . . to their own aspirations, and man began to understand the subjection of all nature with its hidden forces and treasures to himself as a holy duty, imposed upon him by the original ordinances of Paradise: "Have dominion over them." Henceforth, the curse should no longer rest upon the world itself, but upon that which is sinful in it, and instead of monastic flight from the world the duty is now emphasized of serving God in the world in every position of life. To praise God in the Church and serve Him in the world became the inspiring impulse . . . the reconquest of the entire life of the world.[18]

It is time for believers in all the nations to rise up and serve in the spheres of society. . . .

- Christian fathers and mothers need to reclaim the domain of the family and establish it as the pillar of civilization.

- The Church needs to nurture her people and be committed to completing the Great Commission. She needs to train her ranks to be servants and stewards so as to be the salt and light of the earth.

- Believers need to pray for and serve in all levels of government. From the precincts to city hall, from the state legislatures to the White House, the Body of Christ needs to bring the principles of God back into the halls of government.

- Christians must take the lead in education—to launch Christian and home schools, to be salt and light in public institutions, and serve the nation in knowledge and the wisdom that is according to godliness.

- Christian businessmen need to become the world's diplomats; to guide the economic strata in integrity and generosity; and to take dominion over nature for the good of man everywhere.

- The arts must be permeated with godliness and glory; to worship the Creator, and give meaning to creation. Artists must be heroes who point to the Creator, Who is the fountain of all creativity and beauty.

- Believers must take servant leadership in the media, to proclaim the truth and propagate the Gospel; to fill the earth with the knowledge of God as the waters cover the sea.

If the Church of Jesus Christ does not rise to its destiny and exercise servant leadership in the world, then others will continue to fill the void. Someone will exercise leadership. The spheres have been established. The question is *who* will care enough to fill them. At present, sadly, Christians have lost them by default.

We have mentioned seven spheres of authority which guide the affairs of men. When the children of Israel conquered Jericho, they marched around the city seven times and then blew the trumpet of victory. If the people of God will march as servants upon the spiritual strongholds of today, *God* will blow the trumpet and whole nations will be changed for the glory of God.

For too many years the Church has limited the authority of Christ to the four walls of the cathedral. But a new day is dawning. All over the world Christians are awakening to their responsibility to serve people and influence whole nations for the Lord Jesus Christ. This comes from an understanding of sphere sovereignty, a heart of servanthood, and a desire to crown Jesus Lord in all the earth.

God has a plan to turn nations around. He also has a plan to build ones that have never been previously built. Nations *can* be changed. Will the Church have the long-range vision to allow those changes to come?

For Thought and Application

1. What are the seven spheres that mold the character of a nation? What are the primary three, and what sets these apart from the rest?

2. Which of the seven spheres do you think is the most influential in your nation? Why?

3. To which sphere do you feel called to influence for Christ? What can you do to change it? What will it look like if it is molded to God's glory?

4. Prayerfully form a long-range plan to influence your sphere of interest in your nation. Make a list of how you can serve. Believe God to bring change through your life.

David was not a believer in the theory that the world will grow worse and worse, and that the dispensations will wind up with general darkness, and idolatry. Earth's sun is to go down amid tenfold night if some of our prophetic brethren are to be believed. Not so do we expect, but we look for a day when the dwellers in all lands shall learn righteousness, shall trust in the Saviour, shall worship Thee alone, O God, "and shall glorify Thy name." The modern notion has greatly dampened the zeal of the Church for missions, and the sooner it is shown to be unscriptural the better for the cause of God. It neither consorts with prophecy, honors God, nor inspires the Church with ardour. Far hence be it driven.[1]

Charles Spurgeon

SEVEN

OCCUPY UNTIL
I COME

Martin Luther must have been perplexed. He had grown up in the traditionalism of the Roman Catholic world order. In that framework which had dominated Europe for hundreds of years, little seemed to change.

Following his nailing of the 95 Theses on the Wittenberg door, he watched as God birthed a reformation within segments of the Church that totally altered its identity and began to affect whole nations. Massive change was in the air and new hope and excitement.

As he studied the Scripture, Luther was also greatly thrilled with the possibility of Jesus' glorious return to the earth. In light of what God was doing, it seemed that His return was imminent. Wasn't prophecy being fulfilled? Wasn't darkness increasing as the light also burst forth?

So the flamboyant and outspoken Luther seemed to live in tension. The Reformation was building, but so was the darkness, and opposition of the Catholic Church. Jesus was returning. That couldn't be denied. So what was a reformed monk to do?

Sola Scriptura. Believe the Bible alone. What did it say about these things? Luther wasn't sure. So when someone asked him one day about the return of the Lord and the building Reformation, he replied: "Even if I believe that Jesus is returning tomorrow, I will still plant my apple tree today!"

Many of us can identify with Martin Luther. He seemed to be a down-to-earth kind of person who didn't let theology and philosophizing go to his head. He was a brilliant man with an amazing intellect—but he was also a practical man who wanted to live his life by faith in Christ and obey the teachings of the Bible.

Many today are just like Martin Luther. We don't have degrees in theology, but we love Jesus and want to acknowledge Him as Lord of our lives. We can't figure out everything in Scripture, but then we don't have to. The important things make sense, and God's principles do work in everyday life. We are maturing in our faith and want to be lifetime disciples in the real world, growing in grace and knowledge everyday and applying it in our lives.

Many of us would also agree with Martin Luther's approach to Christ's return. The Bible seems to indicate that it could be at any moment. We are excited, and see the signs of the end times all around us. On the other hand we have our IRA, wonder how we're going to put our kids through college, and have perhaps planned a little for our retirement years. That is, if Jesus does not return before then!

We believe that Jesus could return tomorrow. But we are still planting a few apple trees just in case He doesn't.

This dichotomy could be called a "fisherman's approach" to eschatology. (Eschatology relates to the study of the last days, i.e., before Christ's return.) It's practical. It's reasonable. It was probably the theological viewpoint of Peter and all his fisherman friends. What was good for them is good enough for us. After all, didn't they get the very best teachings on eschatology from the Master Himself and still couldn't figure it all out? What they *did* know was that *He was Lord of all the earth*. They gave their lives to that truth and awaited His glorious return.

We live in a day and age in which a great debate is stirring in the Body of Christ over Christian influence in society and the imminent return of Christ. Many books and magazine articles have been written, and sides have quickly polarized into two different camps: On one side is the group highlighting the signs of the times; the growing evil on earth, the coming of the Antichrist, and the imminent rapture of the saints at Christ's return. On the other side are those emphasizing the increasing revival in the Church, the spreading of light in the world, the lordship of Jesus, and the possible long-term aspects of Christ's Kingdom in the nations before His return. In both camps are many variations and finer points of doctrine. But these are the two primary poles.

In the theological world, a number of systems are in tension: One is called premillennialism (Christ will return to the earth before the thousand year reign), and another is called postmillennialism (He will return after a time of great Christian advance in the earth). These terms are not mentioned in the Bible, but those who adhere to them believe that the concepts are. There are other perspectives besides these two, but currently they are not part of the debate.

As we talk about the Church exercising servant leadership in the earth, an immediate question comes to mind: What about the Second Coming? How does my concept of the return of Christ and the reign of His Kingdom affect the way that I will live out my faith on the earth? This is an important question. Our theology does affect our lifestyle. Ideas have consequences. That's why so many are divided over this issue at the moment. The premillenialists believe the postmillenialists are leading the Church into a theocracy and de-emphasis of Christ's return. The postmillenialists believe that the premillenialists are letting the world go to hell in a basket and are denying the true authority of Jesus on this earth. The "pre-mils" believe that the "post-mils" are participating in a seduction of Christianity. The post-mils believe that the pre-mils are propagating a reduction of Christianity.

Let's hope that the controversy does not become destructive. It's not worth fighting over. Martin Luther didn't think so. Premillenial. Postmillenial. Most of us would agree with the man who said that he was a Pan-Millenialist. His theology was that "It would all pan out in the end!"

The best thing to do is to return to the wise and simple balance of the Scriptures. The Bible says a lot about Christ's return, and we need to know that and live our lives according to the truth as we see it. There is even more that the Bible says about what we should do on this earth *until* His return. We should heed that body of truth also and put it into practice. Let's begin by looking at that glorious hope that the Bible refers to as the Second Coming of Christ.

The Second Coming

The are 39 passages in the New Testament (not counting the book of Revelation), that talk about Jesus' return to the earth. This is not a large portion of the New Testament, but it is a significant topic, and one on which many segments of the Early Church based their hope. There are different interpretations and sequences given to try and understand these passages. Some believe in just one Second Coming, while others believe in two or three! Some make a differentiation between the Second Coming of Christ, the Day of the Lord, and the Judgment Day. It is beyond the scope of this chapter to analyze these various scenarios. What I will highlight are the central truths of the Coming of Christ, and then we will compare them with our responsibilities until He comes. That should give us the basic Scriptural focus.

The central truths of Christ's Return

*Jesus **will** return a second time.*

This is our glorious hope. As the disciples watched Jesus ascend into heaven, two angels appeared among them and said, "This same Jesus, who was taken up from you into heaven, will so come in like manner as you saw Him go into heaven" (Acts 1:11). It is a *fact* that Jesus will return. It is recorded a number of times in the Gospels that Jesus Himself said: "Then they will see the Son of Man coming in the clouds with great power and glory. And then He will send His angels, and gather together His elect from the four winds . . ." (Mark 13:26,27).

Paul mentions this fact in a number of His letters, saying, "For the Lord Himself will descend from heaven with a shout, with the voice of an archangel, and with the trumpet of God. And the dead in Christ will rise first. Then we who are alive and remain shall be caught up together with them in the clouds to meet the Lord in the air. And thus we shall always be with the Lord. Therefore comfort one another with these words" (I Thess. 4:16-18). This is our comfort. This is hope. Jesus shall return!

Only the Father knows the time of Jesus' return. It is not for us to know.

That's a humble and necessary starting point. Jesus said, "But of that day and hour no one knows, no, not even the angels of heaven, but my Father only" (Matt. 24:36). If Jesus didn't even know the time of His return, how did we come up with all these timelines and flip charts? Do we know more than He? Just before He ascended into heaven, He reinforced this truth: "It is not for you to know times or seasons which the Father has put in His own authority" (Acts 1:7). He was reminding them to stick to their priorities. Dating His return was not one of them.

Jesus will come unexpectedly.

This makes it even more difficult to predict. Not only is the Father the only one who knows, but He is planning Jesus' return at a time that will be completely unexpected. Jesus Himself said, "The Son of Man is coming at an hour when you do not expect Him" (Matt. 24:44). This was a statement made to believers, not to the world in general. Paul reiterated this when he wrote, "For you yourselves know perfectly that the day of the Lord so comes as a thief in the night" (I Thess. 5:2). Sometimes I wonder how "perfectly" we know that. Is it possible that Jesus' triumphal return will be as unexpected to most of us as His first visit was to the Jews?

We are to be ready at all times for His return.

This seems to be one of the clearest themes of the Second Coming. Jesus told the parable of the Ten Virgins to illustrate it (Matt. 25:1-13). In Luke 12:35-48, He gave a lengthy discourse on the virtue of the righteous slave who was ready for His Master's return. He said, "Therefore you also be ready. . . . Blessed is that servant whom his Master will find so doing when he comes. . . . And that servant who knew his master's will, and did not prepare himself or do according to his will, shall be beaten with many stripes." Perhaps the strongest encouragement that Jesus gave to be ready is found in Mark 13. Here, in three separate admonitions, the Lord says, "Take heed, watch and pray." "Watch, therefore, for you do not know when the Master of the house is coming." And finally, "And what I say to you I say to all: Watch!" I think we should get the point! We are supposed to be watchful and ready for His return.

We are to look for and hasten Christ's Coming.

We are not only to be ready, but we are to be expectant and hopeful, and help bring about the return of Christ. Peter says, "Therefore since all these things will be dissolved, what manner of persons ought you to be in holy conduct and godliness, looking for and hastening the coming of the day of God" (II Peter 3:11, 12). By our godly lives, we can "hasten that day." What a glorious perspective this is, and a privilege to participate. No wonder the cry of the Early Church was, "Maranatha! . . . O Lord come!" (I Cor. 16:22).

Jesus will come to judge and restore the earth.

The coming of Christ is a joy to the believer and the mark of judgment for the lost. Paul says, "When the Lord Jesus is revealed from heaven with his mighty angels, in flaming fire taking vengeance on those who do not know God, and on those who do not obey the Gospel of our Lord Jesus Christ. These shall be punished with everlasting destruction from the presence of the Lord and from the glory of His power" (II Thess. 1:7-9). In Acts 3:20 we are told that the Father will "send Jesus Christ . . . Whom heaven must receive until the times of restoration of all things." Christ's return will condemn the wicked, but for the righteous it will mean the beginning of a new era of restoration and blessing.

Christ's return will be preceded by a number of signs and events.

In the four main passages in the Gospels where Jesus discusses His return (Matt. 24, Mark 13, and Luke 17 and 21), He makes it very plain that some things have to take place *before* He comes again. Though there is much interpretation on some of these points, the basics are clear: There will be "wars and rumors of wars"; "famines and earthquakes"; "persecution"; "the love of many will grow cold"; "the Gospel will be preached in all the world"; "the abomination of desolation" will occur; "great tribulation" will come; "false christs and prophets" will arise; and there will be "signs in the heavens." One thing we are sure of: These things will take place. At some point afterwards, Jesus will return.

These seven points are the definite emphasis of the New Testament regarding the return of Jesus. We know that He is returning. We do not know when, and will probably be surprised. It is for us to be ready, watchful, expectant and hopeful. Jesus will come to gather His elect and execute judgment on the ungodly. He will restore all things. His coming will be preceded by a number of signs and circumstances on the earth.

It is very important to see from Scripture that predicting His return is definitely frowned upon. The Bible makes it abundantly clear that it is for God to know the time — pre-mil, post-mil, or pan-mil! It is for us to be ready and watchful. If we try to figure out all the details of the future we are stepping outside of what God has told us to do. We are to study the Bible. We should cling to the truth as we see it. But in the area of the Second Coming, the Bible encourages us to focus on our character and our responsibilities. That is where we now turn.

Our Responsibilities Until Christ's Return

As we read through the New Testament and get an overview of its contents, we must believe God placed in it the emphasis He desired. In John 21 we read that the whole world could have been filled with books only about the life of Jesus (John 21:25). God was not lacking for material when He inspired the canonization of the books of Scripture. What He gave to us is what He wanted to emphasize. A basic principle of Bible interpretation is, God will give us the most information on what He wants us to focus. Good teaching comes through repetition. What God really wants us to understand, He reminds us of again and again. After all, He knows who we are: depraved human beings who need all the help we can get.

Over 230 passages in the New Testament tell us about our responsibilities as Christians on the earth until Jesus returns in power. This is six times more material than the passages on the Second Coming! God's emphasis is clear: He wants us to focus on our responsibilities, and encourage us to leave the future to Him. It's not that the future does not have importance. It is simply a matter of priority. If we do our part, most certainly God will take care of His (of course He will whether we do so or not). Jesus saved us for a reason, and not primarily to analyze and wait for His return. We have a job to do on the earth. What are those responsibilities? What should be the priorities of every Christian on earth?

Our main priority in life should be to glorify God and bring Him pleasure (John 17:4, Rev. 4:11). But how do we do this? What are we to concentrate on both in hastening and waiting for His return?

Seven areas stand out in the Bible relative to our responsibilities until He returns:

We are to occupy until He comes.

In the parable of the pounds or *minas* (Luke 19:11-27 KJV), which was a picture of Jesus going away and then returning to earth to see if His followers had obeyed Him, the admonition is given to "occupy until I come." The word *occupy* means to do business so as to righteously control land or territory. Jesus does not want us to retreat from the world, but to occupy it—possess it and rule it—just as an occupying army would. The servant who occupied was viewed as the faithful one, whereas the one who did nothing had everything taken away from him.

The role of the Church is to occupy the world for the Lord Jesus Christ. We are to do the business of the Kingdom in proclaiming and demonstrating the Good News of God.

We are to love and obey God.

The first commandment is to "Love the Lord your God with all your heart, with all your soul, and with all your mind" (Matt. 22:37). He is to be the supreme desire of our lives. We are to love no one and no thing more than Him. And love will obey. That's why Jesus said, "If you love Me, you will keep My commandments." Love always obeys, and it obeys in everything. There is nothing that characterizes believers more than obedient love for God. In the Scripture it is equated with being born again (John 3:36).

We are to love and serve one another.

The mark of true Christianity on earth is love for one another. Jesus said, "A new commandment I give to you, that you love one another; as I have loved you, that you also love one another. By this all will know that you are my disciples, if you have love for one another" (John 13:34, 35). This should be a starting point for all those who hold differing eschatological views. How convicting are the true standards of God in these areas! If we practiced this truth, disunity in the Body of Christ would melt away. In I Peter 3:8 we are encouraged to live in harmony, to be compassionate and humble. John tells us flatly that if we do not love our brother, we can't possibly love God (I John 4:20). He says, "We also ought to lay down our lives for the brethren" (I John 3:16). That was Jesus' example — to love us and serve us enough to die for us. We are commanded to do the same.

We are to preach the Gospel to every creature.

The Church was left on earth to evangelize it. A number of times Jesus made it very plain that He would not return until the world had been evangelized. "And the Gospel must first be preached to all the nations (Mark 13:10, Matthew 24:14)." In the Greek, the word for nations is *ethne* meaning "people groups or ethnic groups" (not geo-political entities or nations). The Church has failed to fully obey the Lord Jesus in this area. There are currently over 16,000 unreached *ethnes* in the world, and over 2 billion people who have never heard of Jesus Christ. This is a condition for Christ's return that we are to help fulfill.

We are to preach and extend the Kingdom of God earth.

The message of the Lord Jesus Himself was to announce the coming of the Kingdom of God (Mark 1:15). The majority of His teaching was about that Kingdom, and how it would grow to envelop the entire world like leaven leavening bread. He sent out His disciples to "Preach the kingdom of God and to heal the sick" (Luke 9:2). Just before He left the earth, Jesus instructed His disciples, "speaking of the things pertaining to the kingdom of God" (Acts 1:3). They did so. The focus and burden of the Early Church was "preaching the kingdom of God and teaching the things which concerned the Lord Jesus" (Acts 28:31). The Kingdom was to grow and grow in all the earth until, "the kingdoms of this world have become the kingdoms of our Lord and of His Christ" (Rev. 11:15). This is the primary pursuit of every believer: "Seek first the kingdom of God and His righteousness" (Matt. 6:33).

We are to influence nations and see whole nations come to Christ.

In the Great Commission in Matthew 28:18-20, Jesus says, "All authority has been given to me in heaven and on earth. Go therefore and make disciples of all the nations. . . ." He emphatically states that He has all authority both in heaven and *on earth*. He is the "ruler over the kings of the earth" (Rev. 1:5). He has that authority *now*. It is not something that will come later. This is why He can exhort His followers to make disciples of all nations because His lordship extends over the nations. Paul reiterates this theme of affecting nations when he says that we should bring "nations unto the obedience to the faith" (Rom. 16:26). We are to believe God to affect whole nations in the spreading of the Gospel. This is done through serving the nations in obedience to the lordship of Christ. It does not center around us. It is obedience to who He is.

We are the salt and light of the earth.

Jesus said that we are the seasoner and preserver of the earth. We are also the only light of truth that the world has, and are meant to be a "city set on a hill" (Matt. 5:13-16). We are to shine the light of good works and holy behavior into the world with such impact and clarity that people will respect God even if they do not fully embrace the claims of the Gospel. This speaks of the influence Christians are to have in all of society. Jesus does not say to shine the light only into certain sectors. He says we are the light of the world—the whole world. To the degree that we are salt and light is to the same degree that the world knows right and wrong. We are the gauge of morality and decency. God holds us responsible to be salt and light, and judges *us* if we put our light under a bushel and do not prophetically affect the world's standards.

The largest body of teaching in the New Testament concerns our responsibilities as Christians before Christ returns. Jesus and the New Testament writers made it very plain that the Church had a job to do in the world. We were saved for a purpose. This is our priority—not what God is going to do in the future. He is the Master of the house, and we are His servants. Our responsibility is to obey His orders, not figure out how the whole house is to be run! We are to love and obey Him, love and serve one another, take the Gospel to every creature on earth, extend His kingdom everywhere, occupy the earth until His return, serve and disciple whole nations in His ways, and fulfill our role as the salt and light of the earth. That's what we're to do . . . and leave the rest to Him.

The Balance of the Wise

For most of this century, the Church has been relatively obedient in readying herself for Christ's return. There has been a great emphasis on this in the evangelical world; hundreds of books have been written, and movies have been made. Many have come to know Christ through hearing the message of the Tribulation, the Rapture of the Church, and the imminent return of Christ. This has had its good effect. It has especially been a comfort in lands where believers are suffering for their faith, just as it was in the time of the Early Church. It has also been helpful to sort out the motives of believers. As George Ladd explains:

> The delay of the master made no difference to the true servant: he busied himself about his Lord's business. But the master's delay induced the false servant to a sinful course of action. The Lord's delay brought out the true character of his servants.[2]

The message of *readiness* and *expectancy* is very important. This was the emphasis of Jesus when He taught on His return. We need to listen very carefully to this emphasis and obey it. If we do not, we will be like one of the ten virgins who was invited to the heavenly feast, but never made it in.

On the other hand, we have not obeyed the Lord in our *responsibilities* before His return. This is why we are seeing a shift in many people's practical eschatologies. A number of key biblical truths are beginning to change the life and focus of the Church.

One of these is a renewed focus on the Kingdom of God. This is coming alive in Scripture to many. They are seeing it as much greater, more comprehensive, and more central to the message of the New Testament than ever before. Many are coming to the same conclusion as E. Stanley Jones who wrote a powerful book on the subject. He said:

> To tie up the Kingdom of God with the Second Coming is without Scriptural warrant. To say we can do little or nothing until He comes is to have our light turn to darkness. The Kingdom of God is God's total answer to man's total need now.[3]

Another fresh discovery has been the truth about the authority and lordship of Christ. This is probably the central issue. The Early Church turned the Roman Empire upside down because of their belief that Jesus was Lord—they simply had another King. The Reformation took off in Europe as believers turned to the Bible, and again asserted the supremacy of Christ's lordship on earth right now. They began to see in the Scriptures that Jesus already had *all authority* in heaven and on earth. Bob Mumford shares a tantalizing question on that subject:

> If Jesus has all authority now (Matt. 28:18), then what more authority will He have when He comes?

Others are experiencing for the first time in their Christian lives a rebirth of optimism and hope. Having gone through years of gloom and doom, many are watching a growing revival in the nations of the earth (even in the midst of great persecution and suffering). They are beginning to wonder whether they have been so preoccupied with the

Antichrist and theories of prophecy that they have missed the moving of God's Spirit. The encouraging signs around them —which are many—and the fact that many prophetical books have already proven to be false, have nudged them towards thinking that it's at least possible God is not done with the earth yet! That perhaps some showers of blessing are still going to fall before history is over. And so faith has been building in their hearts, and an openness to believe that they might need to think long-range and/or live out their lifetimes. Gary North states it this way:

> We are seeing a shift in practical eschatology. It now includes a vision of victory.

> Better to plan for a long-term program to subdue the whole earth, generation by generation, than to squander our capital in a short-term sprint to save a remnant and then leave the world to the devil. Aim high, aim carefully, and shoot long.[4]

Some are beginning to see the extremely negative consequences of living every day as if it were our last, as if Christ were coming at any moment. If we are consistent with that view, then it can easily lead to doing very little to change our world, and to do little if any long-range planning. And those who do no long-range planning can never lead. This brings us to a disturbing thought:

What would creation have been like if God had lived for only His "last" creative day?

Answer: We would have man (and animals) living in total darkness.

Is that the kind of world we are creating by not having a long-range orientation? Are we saving men's souls, but leaving them to live and move in a world of total darkness?

The emphasis of the Bible is clear. We are to be *ready* and excited about the glorious return of the Lord Jesus. Until that wonderful day, we are *responsible* to proclaim and demonstrate the Gospel through our service among the nations of the earth. We are to avoid both fatalism and end-time speculation. Both will lead us into error. On the contrary, we must wholeheartedly do the will of God in the empowering of the Holy Spirit. God will ultimately determine the future according to His wise timetable.

What Are We To Do?

Martin Luther isn't the only one who lived in a perplexing time. In our day, storm clouds of darkness and evil are gathering on the horizon. At the same time, God is awakening His people to extend His rulership into the nations of the earth. The future could hold greater judgments or the dawn of a new, exciting era.

What are we to do?

Occupy until He comes. Search the Scriptures. Love God and one another. Obey Him and do His will. Look in readiness for the coming of the Lord from heaven. Fulfill His commands on the earth. We do not need to hold to a particular view of the future to embrace a working concept of Christ's lordship in the world.

Martin Luther had the right idea. Keep looking up, and keep planting apple trees. Maybe that's why God used him to help bring reformation that has lasted for over 400 years.

For Thought and Application

1. Which does the Scripture emphasize more, the Second Coming of Christ or our responsibilities before His return? Why is this so?

2. Does our concept of His return or of the last days affect the way we live day-to-day? What are the good effects? What are some of the bad?

3. What is your personal belief about the Second Coming? Are you still making long-range plans and goals for yourself, your family and your ministry? How will your view affect your leadership?

4. Meditate on the Scriptures about Christ's return and our responsibilities until He comes. Praise Him for His glorious return. Set your heart to occupy until He comes.

You have a world to win!

Karl Marx
Communist Manifesto

Stand firm in your faith and fear Allah, so that you may triumph.

Mohammed
The Koran

Go into all the world and preach the Gospel to every creature.

The Lord Jesus Christ
The Bible

EIGHT

THE BATTLE FOR WORLD LEADERSHIP

A young, zealous, French Marxist once wrote the following sobering letter to a friend who had become a Christian:

> The Gospel is a much more powerful weapon for the renewal of society than is our Marxist philosophy, but all the same it is we who will finally beat you. We are only a handful and you Christians are numbered by the millions. But if you remember the story of Gideon and his three hundred companions, you will understand why I am right. . . . We Communists do not play with words. We are realists and seeing that we are determined to achieve our objective we know how to obtain the means.
>
> Of our salaries and wages we keep only what is strictly necessary, and we give the rest for propaganda purposes. To this propaganda we also "consecrate" all of our free time, and part of our holidays. You, however, give only a little time and hardly any money for the spreading of the Gospel of Christ. How can anyone believe in the supreme value of this Gospel, if you do not practice it, and if you sacrifice neither time nor money for it?
>
> Believe me, it is we who will win, for we believe in our Communist message and are willing to sacrifice everything, even our life, in order that social justice may triumph. But you people are afraid to soil your hands.[1]

This young Marxist knew something of which most people on earth are totally oblivious. He knew a great battle is taking place for the hearts and minds of men and nations. He knew it was a battle worth fighting, and worth winning.

There is a great contest going on for the prize of world leadership. This has always been true because of the two competing kingdoms, but today it has come down to a war between a number of competing world views. The winner of this battle will lead the twenty-first century.

As Christians, we need to understand we are in a war and commit ourselves to the army of the Lord Jesus Christ. The war is well underway, and many troops have taken the field. But the outcome is far from settled.

World Views in Conflict

Abraham Kuyper said near the turn of this century that there were five primary world views battling for supremacy on earth. There are, of course, many more religions and philosophies than that—but Mr. Kuyper believed that the majority fit into one of five categories:

- Paganism (Pantheism)
- Islam
- The Institutional Church
- Modernism (Humanism)
- Biblical Christianity

Dr. Kuyper believed that these religions or philosophies encompass all of humanity. At least these five are the most powerful forces for the development of culture and change that exist in the world. They all have a distinct concept of man's three basic relationships: Man's relationship to God, his relationship to other men, and his relationship to the physical world. Let's take a brief look at these five world views. Their concepts give birth to a myriad of consequences.

Paganism—This primarily Eastern concept of reality teaches that God is actually *in* nature, making all gods and human beings part of the "divine." This is classic pantheism, and gives birth to a panorama of idolatry as evidenced in the Far East, among American Indians and African tribes. In this framework some men rise to become "god-men" (*maharishis*, or the *buddha*), and in ancient cultures were known to rise to a place of divine despotism (as in Egypt, Greece, Rome, India, and Japan). Regarding the world, since divinity is found in nature, any development of resources and the environment is upsetting the "divine ecology." Progress and development are discouraged and the result is often poverty and backwardness.

Islam—The Islamic view of life teaches that there is a God (Allah) that rules all of life, but he is distant and distinct from his creation. The Moslem religion has a generally low view of man, and believers are encouraged to subjugate, forcibly convert, and even exterminate unbelievers as an act of worship to Allah. There is little individual conscience nor human rights. Women are inferior to men, and subjugated to them. The Islamic idea of the world is an environment to be conquered, not developed. For this reason, most Moslem nations were undeveloped and, before the discovery of oil, some of the most impoverished nations on earth.

The Institutional Church—This strongly hierarchal view of Christianity teaches that the Church is the mystical link between God the Creator and His creation. As the source of God's revelation on earth, only the Church can accurately interpret God's ways and designs in history. This tends to produce a hierarchy among men, with a class of priests, bishops, and pontiffs giving leadership at the top. It also helped produce the concept of the divine right of kings and the state church structures which became prominent in Europe. In this view, the world and the Church are in total conflict which will not be resolved until the coming of Christ's future and perfect kingdom. This over-emphasis of the hereafter tends to create a large feudal class, and does not encourage much development in this present sinful world.

Modernism—This is the modern tree of atheism with its branches of humanism and Marxism. God is dead, and man is alone in the universe to rise to leadership and divinity. He must be his own savior. Men are all equal (except in Marxism where some men are more equal than others), and there is no God to raise up some and put others down. This is the role of the state, either through humanistic democracy, socialism, or the total authoritarianism of communism. In this view the world has been constantly and randomly evolving, and needs radical change through revolution to aid it along. Revolution *is* progress and development, regardless of the effects on the physical world.

Biblical Christianity—This is the non-institutional approach to Christianity as revealed in the Scriptures and seen in the life of many Bible-believing movements. God the Creator and His creation are historically linked through Christ, existentially brought together by the Holy Spirit, and intellectually linked through the Bible. God is available to every believer. Men are all equal before God and His Word, and many authorities or jurisdictions have been given to create harmony and freedom. Regarding the world, man is responsible for culture, and is to bring all aspects of the world under Christ's lordship.

It is within these world views, or as Dr. Kuyper called them—life-systems—that the battle for Planet Earth has been waging. Every once in a while a new offshoot comes into existence (like the twentieth century phenomenon of Marxism-Communism), but the roots have been there for eons. Despite their great differences, each of these world views produces a comprehensive orientation toward life. Dr. Kuyper came to the conclusion that if true Christianity were to win the war for the minds of men (world evangelism) it needed to be taught and lived out as a total way of life—not a half-baked philosophy tucked away in the religious cubbyhole of the mind. To triumph it had to be true. To be true, it had to be more powerful and comprehensive than the rest. Comparing it to the assault of modernism, he proclaimed:

If the battle is to be fought with honor and with a hope of victory, then principle must be arrayed against principle; then it must be felt that in Modernism the vast energy of an all-embracing life-system assails us, then also it must be understood that we have to take our stand in a life-system of equally comprehensive and far-reaching power.[2]

It had to be the truth of the Bible lived out in every dimension of life. Then and only then would it be worthy to compete in the battle of the times.

The Essentials of a Victorious World View

In pondering these different life-systems, their appeal and historical effectiveness, one comes to the conclusion that each of these world views has a portion of truth, borrowed or perverted from Biblical Christianity. That is why they succeed at all. After all, it is only God's truths that work. But sinful man can take them as principles and apply them for selfish gain. The good things of God can be used wrongly by men, but even then, the strengths of the principles themselves will shine through, despite the evil of the motive involved.

There are principles of leadership and principles of victory. To the degree that a religion or philosophy lives out those truths, its world view will rise to prominence in human affairs. Let us now look at these essential ingredients:

First of all, a victorious world view must be able to provide a sense of destiny and hope. It has to be able to look into the future and offer its adherents a plan of victory and a spiritual sense of the inevitability of its cause. It has to be seen as progressive, and that which offers the greatest amount of hope and purpose to the individual or society. Ray Sutton explains:

The major ideologies of the world have all held to some concept of destiny: Christianity, Islam, Marxism. All three implicitly espouse a doctrine of destiny. That is, each person believes that the world belongs to him, and that someday the world will be dominated by his religion.[3]

Without this concept of destiny, a philosophy would not be viewed as worthy of extensive propagation. And the spreading of its message to many others is central to its plan to conquer the world. This belief in inevitable triumph builds momentum and power.

Secondly, a victorious life-system must inspire a great degree of zeal, commitment, and character, especially under trying circumstances. Without the strength of a strong ethical base, it cannot begin to accomplish its task. The world is a big place and there are many obstacles to overcome. So a triumphant world view must create in its people a willingness to sacrifice, work tirelessly, and have the strength of character to achieve its goals. Commitment of character becomes the ultimate advantage in any war of competing ideologies. In most cases, those who want victory the most will rise to possess it. This is the law of labor and discipline. A successful world view must find a way to make its goal appear worthy of sacrifice unto victory.

Thirdly, a victorious world view needs to find strength and continuity in a written absolute. It needs to have a "book" or manifesto to guide its development. It cannot span generations without a written ideal that makes its way into hearts and minds. This guiding "revelation" must stand the test of time and scrutiny. A written manifesto is an essential source of strength and continuance. Without it, the emotions can die and the passions be lost. A world view needs a foundation that is perceived to be "true," and this always takes a written form.

There are other elements important to a victorious world view, but I believe that these three—destiny, character, and a written absolute—are the most foundational and essential. In the end, the world view *must work* to be victorious, (but this is not essential to its primary spreading and initial effectiveness).

In light of these observations, let's examine the world views battling for worldwide leadership.

Paganism

Pantheism and its many offshoots have millions of adherents worldwide. However, pantheism lacks any sense of destiny. Life is seen as a continual cycle or wheel. It is hard to maintain zeal for the propagation of a philosophy without a clear vision of triumph. The one exception is the New Age version of pantheism, which believes in an Aquarian destiny controlled by the stars.

Paganism by definition contains so many gods that it is difficult to verify its accuracy and absolutes. Its *primary absolute* is that *there are no absolutes*, and you cannot build strong character and culture around *non-ideas*. The lack of character it produces will be its ultimate downfall. Yoga and meditation do not produce zeal, commitment, and sacrifice (some notable exceptions to this are the Japanese versions which combined a deep sense of nationalism, and Zen Buddhist training which includes extreme discipline in personal asceticism). Paganism will always have adherents, but they will be there more for fascination and pleasure than for discipline and triumph. Paganism cannot rival for world dominion. It lacks the character to get there.

The Institutional Church

Likewise, the institutional church will not rise to major leadership in coming years. Those years of supremacy and her perceived infallibility are behind, and many nations have been left with a very dry taste in their mouths. The church as an institution possesses the "Book" that contains a sense of destiny, power for character, and is her written absolute. But her mystical understanding of relationship to Christ, and her relegation of the Bible to the priesthood have curtailed her power. As to the conflict with the world, the church has given up, and rather placidly awaits the return of Christ's Kingdom. This lack of vision and practical power condemns the religious to a life of either asceticism or mediocrity.

Humanism

Humanism and Marxism could be put under the term "Modernism." They are the same in philosophy but differ in methods. Marxism is humanism enforced with the barrel of a gun. That is the only real difference. Given enough time, humanism always produces totalitarian forms, as shown by the example of the French Revolution. Humanism is the parent of Marxism-Leninism. Humanism in the West has been forced to "stay young." If given the opportunity to "grow up," she would most certainly adopt many methods of her children.

Humanism, or secularism, is the fundamental world view of contemporary Western democracies. It has its roots in the Enlightenment of the 1700s, but has only risen to prominence in what Francis Schaeffer has called the Post-Christian Era. Most Western nations have separated God and religion from their public life. Atheism is the religion of public consciousness.

Humanism has a sense of destiny—it believes that it has arrived on the historical scene as the vehicle of progress. It sees itself as champion of the new age to come, leading the world into a higher civilization. Many books assert its essential premises. Its basic documents are the *Humanist Manifestos I & II*, which have been signed by some of the West's leading intellectuals. James Reichley says of the power of this world view:

> Despite many ups and downs, the influence of secular civil humanism in the West since the Enlightenment has generally followed an ascending course. Even in the United States, where religion remains a powerful social force, civil humanism is now probably the dominant value system within the intellectual community. It thereby exerts strong influence over the entertainment and news industries and over the higher levels of the education system and the government bureaucracy.[4]

Notice how humanism has taken over Western societies. It brought its ideas into the power structures — entertainment, news industries, higher education, and government — that mold the minds of individuals and nations. Its adherents moved into positions of influence in the areas of sphere sovereignty. Gary DeMar rightly comments that, "The advance of humanism is the result of the retreat of Christianity. Just as a neglected garden will be overwhelmed by weeds, so a neglected area of responsibility will be overwhelmed by evil."[5]

"Practical humanists" (atheists, agnostics, or Christians who believe that they must not bring their faith into the public arena), are in the driver's seat. They have earned their position through the default of Biblical Christians.

There is one great problem with humanism. Its principles and policies do not work, and the further we go, the more that is evident. Monstrous problems today in economics, the breakdown of the family, alcoholism, drug abuse, youth rebellion, increasing mental illness, and venereal disease, must be laid at the doorstep of humanism. As a religion and philosophy, humanism has failed, and we are surrounded by its wreckage.

The main reason for this failure is that humanism lacks one essential ingredient: It cannot produce righteous character, and without this element, it cannot survive. James Reichley summarizes this:

> The fundamental flaw of secular civil humanism as a basis for democratic values is that it fails to meet the test of intellectual credibility. . . . Using purely natural criteria, either the self or society must finally be regarded as sovereign. If the self, a rational individual will honor only those social values that serve his fairly immediate selfish interests. If society, personal freedom and the rights of individuals are left at the mercy of established secular authority. In either case, democracy lacks essential moral support.[6]

It is the lack of this moral support and hence, intellectual honesty, that is bringing the West to the precipice of ruin. Other nations may try its materialistic ways, but they will discover the party cannot last. Every humanistic civilization is doomed to die by eating itself up with self-indulgence.

This is why humanism will not be in the final race for world leadership. It will put up a valiant three-quarters, but on the final lap it will tire and fade from the track. At that point humanism's loyal adherents will turn to another to lead on to victory. It could be its closest of kin—Marxism.

If neither pantheism nor humanism have the elements for success, that leaves three major ideologies which will battle for the destiny of the planet. They are active now, but the years of hottest battle are ahead.

Marxism

In the past seventy years, the world view of Marxism-Leninism has risen to supremacy in over half the inhabited world. More than two billion people live under its all-embracing life-system. Not everyone in these nations believe its claims, but nonetheless it guides the public life of a vast number of people.

It is a formidable foe with one agenda: to dominate and rule the world. I have been in over ten Marxist nations, and it has never ceased to amaze me how clear and how unified its message is: "Workers of the world unite!" is emblazoned on office and schoolroom walls, billboards—everywhere! In the Soviet Union, the ever-present photos of Marx, Lenin, and Engels are its icons. And everywhere world maps and globes are displayed—with the sickle and hammer emblazoned in prophetic triumph.

Karl Marx's godless philosophy was a reaction to the decadence of the Church of his time. The following is his own bitter indictment:

> The social principles of Christianity have had eighteen
> centuries in which to develop, and have no need to under-

go further development. . . . The social principles of Christianity assume there will be no compensation in heaven for all the infamies committed on earth, and thereby justify the persistence of infamies here below. The social principles of Christianity are lickspittle [spit], whereas the proletariat is revolutionary. So much for the social principles of Christianity![7]

Marxism as a world view contains all the necessary elements to compete in the battle for the world. It has a clear sense of destiny, inspires sacrifice to achieve its goals, and bases its philosophy squarely on the pen of its founder. The writings of Karl Marx and his followers are the bible of the communist world. *The Communist Manifesto* has been the 95 Theses of the twentieth century, but instead of bringing righteous reform, it has caused many bloody and costly revolutions. The French Revolution was the first bloodbath of atheism. But Marxism-Communism has taken it on to perfection.

Gary North compares Marxism with Christianity in four points:

> Communist theory possesses all four of the most prominent features of future-oriented Christianity. Christianity offers a four-point system of *progress*, *providence*, *ethics*, and the self-attesting truth of *the Bible*. Communists imitate this system and thereby gain the minds of men who seek relief from the cursed world of sin. [Italics mine]

> First, they have a doctrine of progress. The hope of man is in the successful revolution. The proletariat will be triumphant in history. Those who ally themselves with Communism . . . have allied themselves with victory.

> Second, they have a doctrine of providence. This providence is impersonal, unlike Christianity's providence of God. The Marxist providence is historical, the dialectical process. . . . This is a doctrine of predestination, which undergirds their hope in the future. There is no escape from the materialistic forces of history. Each stage in historical development is inevitable.

Third, they have a doctrine of ethical law. Each stage of historical development produces its appropriate ethics and philosophy. Since the proletarian stage of Communism is the final stage, proletarian ethics is also final . . . it is ultimate . . . it is a tool of social transformation.

Fourth, they have a doctrine of self-authenticating philosophy. . . . Marxism does not need to appeal to a common ground philosophy of being. There is no common ground; there is no common being; there is only becoming — revolutionary action — until the victory of the proletarians.

Because Communist theory can offer this comprehensive vision of secular salvation for society, it can compete successfully with Christianity.

Marxism is the most consistent and powerful secular religion of all time; it can only be successfully challenged by an even more consistent and more powerful Biblical religion.[8]

In the twentieth century, there has been no more formidable opponent to the Kingdom of God than Marxism. It has proclaimed an inevitable future victory, worked hard to achieve its goals, and captured nation after nation through persuasion, then manipulation and brute force. It hurls Nikita Khrushchev's challenge in the face of Western nations: "We will bury you!" It then quietly and methodically works "détente-tively" to achieve global conquest.

Yet the cracks of the empire are beginning to show. This is primarily because the world has had seventy years to observe the results of this world view. It is not very pretty. There has also been time to analyze the message of its authorities, and that too has come up wanting. Gary North continues:

What Communism has produced is an endless series of crop failures. In Communist China, it took only two years of partial free market agriculture to make that nation an exporter of food, 1983-85, after four decades of starvation. Communism is also the most efficient producer of bureaucratic inefficiency in history. It produces bumper crops of cynicism and corruption. Communist nations systematically and deliberately corrupt their populations. Guilt-ridden, corrupt populations are easier to control.

The Communists know that they can compete with the West only in terms of sheer military and terrorist power. Those are their specialty exports in the world economy.[9]

No area has shown communism's failure more clearly than nations in the Pacific Rim. Here, a great warfare is going on for the destiny of some of the largest nations on earth. It is not going well for the Marxist-Leninists. David Aikman, a long-time correspondent with *TIME* magazine, and a Ph.D. in Russian and Chinese culture, shares in his excellent book, *Pacific Rim*:

> Marxism has been the great philosophical and economic failure of the century as a model for capital formation and the raising of living standards. Wherever it has been the reigning new religion, political and cultural freedoms have also suffered lamentably. There is no more powerful a demonstration of this fundamental observation about differing world views than in the Pacific Rim. Vietnam and Thailand, North and South Korea, China and Taiwan: the comparisons are embarrassing for doctrinaire socialists.[10]

As a philosophy that produces nothing but arms, terrorism, and misery, Marxism-Leninism may soon be in retreat.

Communism is a very subtle perversion of many Christian ideas. Allan Bloom comments, "Marx denied the existence of God but turned over all His functions to History, which is inevitably directed to a goal fulfilling of man and which takes the place of Providence."[11] Thus, communism is the ultimate in naiveté.

Many people are becoming disillusioned with Marxism because of well-reasoned Christian and secular scrutiny.

The editor of the *Washington Kiplinger Letter* makes this observation about the future of Marxism and its relationship to the Information Age:

> At the center of every controlled society sits a government that fears for its stability if the people know too much about the outside world. . . . The controlled societies are going to be left in the dust of the information revolution. Our own intellectual freedoms allow vast numbers of our citizens to be part of that revolution and to use information in new and creative ways. . . . Only an open society such as ours can take full advantage of the new technology. And this will lead to unprecedented growth.
>
> Controlled societies can either join up or fall behind. China seems to be moving in the direction of more openness for its citizens, even adopting a new copyright law based on our own. Will the Soviets join the twentieth century before it becomes the twenty-first? And could they do so without allowing the healthful virus of individual freedom to infect their society?[12]

Yet Marxism remains a religious world view with which to be reckoned. As our young French friend reminded us at the beginning, there are still many people on the planet who believe in its inevitable victory and are willing to pay a sacrificial price to attain it.

And there is yet one other non-Christian world view that is rising in force to accomplish world conquest.

Islam

One of the most ominous signs of the coming battle for world leadership has been the rapid growth of militant Islam. With the Ayatollah Khomeini coming to power in Iran, a whole new wave of Islamic fervor has crested into many nations of the world. Fueled by both oil revenues and the decadence of the Western nations, the Moslem world view is making inroads into nations and cultures. Over 890 million people now adhere to the Islamic religion, and today it is growing faster than most religions.

Islam is a participant in the global contest because it has one of the most pervasive life systems known to man. It includes a clear sense of destiny—the goal of conquering the earth; a fanatical commitment to that cause (even "gloriously unto death," as in the many Shiite suicide missions, and waves of human sacrifice in the Iran-Iraq War); and a written authority that has stood the test of time, the *Koran*. These and other attributes make it a formidable foe. Gary North makes the comparison:

> We think of Islam. It, too, has the shadows of the four points. For predestination they substitute fatalism. For a coming spiritual kingdom on earth they substitute military conquest and (in Iran today) revolution. For Biblical law they substitute *Khadi* justice—the law of the mullahs, God speaking to them directly in the midst of changing historical circumstances. . . . For the self-attesting Bible they substitute a self-attesting Koran. Thus they have also become historically victorious rivals to Christianity.[13]

In many ways the Islamic world view is a greater challenge to real Christianity than Marxism-Leninism. It combines a total life philosophy with the spiritual tie of religion. There is a belief in the supremacy of Allah *and* the willingness to create human revolution on earth to achieve Allah's will. This world view is loaded with religious conviction. Abraham Kuyper writes:

> Even in Islam you find the same power of a conviction of life dominated by one principle. Protestantism alone wanders about in the wilderness without aim or direction, moving hither and thither, without making any progress. . . . Why did we constantly lose ground? Simply because we were devoid of an equal unity of life-conception such as alone could enable us with irresistible energy to repel the enemy at the frontier.[14]

In the battle for world leadership, Islam has already staked out its claim. It is currently experiencing a religious revival that is sending out missionaries into all the earth. They offer a sense of destiny and hope; a cause worthy of sacrifice, even death; and the claims of the Arabic scriptures. They desire to envelope the world in a total way of thinking and a total submission. With this vision and commitment, they are succeeding in many places.

The great weakness of Islam is also found in the fruit of its philosophy. With a low view of man, an even lower view of woman, and a careless disregard for the physical earth, Islam has always resulted in poverty and suffering. With the exception of the oil-producing nations, Islamic nations have a very low standard of living. Even their physical environment is barren and unproductive. Their deserts seem to reflect their world view. The God of Islam is harsh and distant, and his earthly kingdom takes on the arid characteristics of his proposed nature.

Nonetheless, the world view and lifestyle of Islam is a power in the earth today. Its methods are similar to Marxism in both the use of violence and popular revolution (primarily in its militant Shiite form). But Islam comes to power in clerical robes. Because of this, it exudes an aura of double authority.

Biblical Christianity

The third world view with the potential of shaping men and nations is true Christianity. We will refer to this as Biblical Christianity because its vitality is directly linked to the Church conforming to the true message of the Bible: That Jesus Christ came to redeem all peoples, and in His Spirit and authority the Gospel has gone forth to change the world.

The tragedy is, Biblical Christianity has only rarely been practiced in two thousand years. The Early Church moved in the all-encompassing power of the resurrected Lord, and because of their influence, eventually the Roman

Empire bowed to the King of kings and Lord of lords. But soon the Church became institutionalized and enchained in idolatry and medieval religiosity.

During the Middle Ages there were a number of movements that tried to promote a return to the Bible, but it remained for the Reformation to bring Christianity back to a place of ascendancy and life. This rebirth had everything to do with the Scriptures being made available to the common man, and the Bible once again becoming the Book that gave perspective to all life and thought. Jesus was once again viewed as the Lord and King of Heaven *and* earth, and His message of victory began to free whole nations from oppression.

Calvinism especially applied Biblical Christianity and its comprehensive life-message to affect whole nations. Governments were reestablished upon the basis of God's Word; schools and universities were established to "train up the children in the way they should go"; commerce began to reflect the principles of stewardship, thrift, and philanthropy; science blossomed as men and women explored the wonders of the Creator's universe; the arts returned to realism, and expressions of godly creativity; and in many other areas of life, first in Europe and then in America, the seeds of a Biblical Christian civilization sprang up with increasing freedom, prosperity and justice. A world view had taken hold of the reins of many nations. Its fountain was the Bible. Its King was the Lord Jesus.

What the Biblical Christian world view offered was the necessary ingredients for a victorious world view and the proof of its validity in its results. Christianity was true. Christianity worked. It altered history.

It is still true today if we dare to practice it. What we have lost over hundreds of years has been our comprehensive world view that centers on the lordship of Jesus Christ. Through His victorious death and resurrected glory, Jesus Christ alone possesses the power of world deliverance and redemption. Contained in the Bible is God's prescription for triumph. It is up to His people as His servants to apply it to the world.

Biblical Christianity possesses the clearest sense of destiny and hope. The Bible tells us where history is going. It reveals the wonders of the Son of God, and how He was sent to deliver man from the power of the devil. Our real destiny is triumph and our real hope is glory! Our future is not based on a lie or a hoped-for result. It has already been determined and the power has been given to fulfill it on earth. The authority of the Lord Jesus Christ both in this life and the next makes our faith a certainty. Thus Christianity is worthy of propagation because its message is true and has the only power to rescue men and nations from their sins.

It also uniquely possesses the power to inspire zeal and commitment, and also to produce character. There is a Savior who has conquered life and death. "Worthy is the Lamb to receive the due reward of His sufferings." This becomes the rallying cry of the people of God, and with their eyes upon their Lord, they go forth to reap in the earth. There *is* a cause worthy of total sacrifice — a cause to live and die for. As the missionary statesman C. T. Studd once exclaimed, "If Jesus Christ be God and died for me, then no sacrifice will be too great for me to make for Him."

The glorious mystery of the Christian faith is the willingness of God to share His very being and character with those who are reconciled to Him. Only in Christianity is the problem of sin dealt with in the human heart. Through repentance and faith in Christ, the guilt of sin is washed away. And then, God doesn't leave us to just follow Jesus' example of righteousness. The living God comes and imparts His very life into us. The strength of true righteous character is produced by the indwelling Spirit of God. This is not the character of example — it is the power of God operating directly in the life of the believer. Christianity is "Christ in you, the hope of glory" (Colossians 1:27, 28).

And Biblical Christianity has an infallible book to heed. It is the Book of books, the world's all-time bestseller — the

Bible. Our vision in life does not have to be clouded. The Bible tells us where we have come from, God's plans for the present, and the future. Within its pages are a total discovery of life, vitality, power, and meaning. It has been open to scrutiny for two thousand years and has stood the test of time. "The Word of God abides forever." The atheist Voltaire once boasted that the Bible would fade from memory in his lifetime. After he died his home was used to house a printing press that produced Bibles!

Finally, Christianity offers a proof that none of the other world views can—its principles *work*. Biblical Christianity has been the handmaiden of progress because only Christianity teaches that God made men to be stewards over the earth. The earth is not divine; neither is it to be abused nor left undeveloped. It was created to be cultivated and developed by man. Thus it is in the Christian West that science, industry, and the arts have flourished. Material prosperity and republican forms of government with human rights and liberties have also resulted. The world may not recognize the source of all these blessings, but the voice of history is clear: It is the product of Biblical Christianity.

And there is one clear difference between the world views of Biblical Christianity, Marxism, and Islam: Because the latter two are based on deception, they must resort to force to achieve their ends. Their victory can only be pursued with a bayonet and a gun. However this is not true of Biblical Christianity. It enriches the world by serving through love and influence. It manifests the spirit and principles of its God. It achieves power in the same style through which it rules—non-coercive servant leadership. Christianity is not afraid of the marketplace of ideas. It knows truth will prevail—even in a world scarred by the effects of sin.

The Battle For World Leadership

As we near the twenty-first century, the battle lines are drawn. Three major religion-philosophies . . .

- Marxism

- Islam

- and Biblical Christianity

. . . are in mortal combat for supremacy on earth. A war is being waged for the hearts and minds of the billions who must choose. Everyone must choose. The further we go, the narrower the choices will become.

We are living in what may be the Church's finest hour. Though the polarization is great, and problems are multiplying the world over, we have the opportunity to take the message of Christ into all the earth by way of service, love, and in glory. To do so, we must rise up as biblical Christians and present the claims of the Lord Jesus Christ to every dimension of life and to every person on earth.

Biblical Christianity—the seeking of the true Kingdom of God on earth as it is in Heaven—is the answer to the needs of the hour. This has always been true, but many of us have not seen it as a comprehensive world view that alone can enrich the earth.

A generation ago, this lack of understanding had a staggering result. Listen to this amazing story told by the great Methodist preacher, Dr. E. Stanley Jones:

> I was speaking in a cathedral in West Germany on the Kingdom of God. On the front seats were prominent German leaders. As I spoke they kept pounding their benches with their fists. I was puzzled. I did not know what it meant—was it for me or against me? But at the close they revealed what the beating of the benches meant: "You seem to sense why we turned to Nazism. Life for us was at loose ends-compartmentalized. We needed something to bring life back into wholeness, into total meaning and goal. We thought Nazism could bring that wholeness. But it let us down, let us down in blood and ruin. . . . We now see that what we were seeking for was the kingdom of God, but we didn't know it. That's why we pounded the benches, we missed the kingdom of God."

That opened my eyes. I saw in a flash the meaning of these various revolts—the totalitarian revolts, the revolts of youth, the revolt of the races. Are they not all seeking for the Kingdom of God and don't know it? The answer is yes. . . . Some day it will dawn upon them and then we will have the greatest spiritual awakening that this planet has ever seen. For men need nothing so much as they need an absolute from which they can work out to the relativisms of the hour—some master light of all their seeing.[15]

They missed the Kingdom of God, and a world was plunged into war. In the coming mighty battle, will we as biblical Christians so reveal Christ's Kingdom to the earth that the results will be quite different?

First we must understand there is a battle. Next we must be committed to fighting it in the spirit and methods of our Servant King. And finally, we must believe that we can win through the power of the Lord Jesus Christ.

For Thought and Application

1. Can you remember the five primary world views? How are they different from one another? Are there any others?

2. What are the essentials of a victorious world view? Why are these things important? Why will neither humanism nor the New Age movement ever become dominant world views?

3. Why are Biblical Christianity, Marxism, and Islam the most powerful world views in the world today? How are Marxism and Islam similar? In what ways is Biblical Christianity totally different in its methods and style of leadership?

4. Study carefully the essentials of a victorious world view. Apply those truths in your own Christian life. Share them with others.

The inhabitants of many cities, and of many countries, yea, many people and strong nations; great multitudes in different parts of the world . . . shall be given much of a spirit of prayer . . . that He would appear for the help of His Church, and in mercy to mankind, and pour out His Spirit, revive His work, and advance His spiritual kingdom in the world as He has promised . . . which at length will gradually be introduced a revival of religion. . . . And in this manner religion shall be propagated, til the Awakening reaches those that are in the highest stations, and til whole nations be awakened. . . . til at length many people and strong nations shall join themselves to them; and there shall, in process of time, be a vast turning to the Church, so that it shall be ten times as large as it was before; yea, at length, all nations shall be converted unto God. And thus that shall be fulfilled Psalm 65:2: "O Thou that hears prayer, unto Thee shall all flesh come."[1]

Jonathan Edwards

NINE

GOALS AND GREATNESS

Because of our ministry's presence on Capitol Hill, I have been invited to sit in on a number of meetings held by political and religious interest groups. Whether they were conferences, committee meetings, or strategy sessions, most have been disappointing for the lack of one little three-letter word. It is almost never used in discussions. Yet it's an important word—it will be probably the one word God asks of every human being on Judgment Day concerning our lives and actions. That word is *why*.

Why? It's a simple question, but its answer reveals either the beauty of greatness or the ugliness of selfishness. Why are we doing what we are doing? That's the critical question . . .

. . . for a government leader to ask, as billions and billions of dollars are spent, day in and day out.

. . . that every organization should constantly weigh as it generates a product or provides a service.

. . . for each of us to carefully examine in our thoughts, words, and deeds.

Why? Many people don't realize that this little three-letter word could determine their entire future, and reveal whether they are truly in right relationship to God. We tend to concentrate on *what* and *how* and *when* and *where*; for some reason we do not like to look at *why*.

But *why* is the most important question. It is the revelation of who we really are. That is sometimes embarrassing to admit, so we don't ask the question, and just continue the *whats*.

As we look at servant leadership, this question of *why* is utterly crucial. We may not be handling billions of dollars, but we will be making an impact on billions of souls. What is our motive in wanting to lead? What is our true goal in making disciples of all nations?

Goals and Greatness

Some time ago I was thinking about what made a person or a movement great in history. I knew what the world thought. The press uses the word *great* to describe almost anybody who is well-known. Marx was considered a great thinker; Mao Tse-tung and Vladimir Lenin are often described as great leaders; Elvis Presley and Marilyn Monroe were great stars of the screen and stage. But were these people truly "great"? Is greatness simply achieving a certain level of skill or arriving at public notoriety?

Greatness is a concept we must define from God's point of view. True greatness involves at least three attributes.

First, a great person is one who has a worthy goal in life. This eliminates most people. The motive of life, or what a person is living for, must have intrinsic or eternal value. If it does not, nothing that person does should be considered in the category of greatness. To be great, he must begin with a cause that is righteous and worthy and set his sights on achieving it.

Next, the person who aspires to greatness must use righteous means to achieve his goal. A worthy end does not justify an ungodly means. Sometimes people can have a worthy cause, but stoop to low measures to accomplish their objectives. This is not greatness, but a pragmatism that compromises principle.

And lastly, a great person needs to persevere under trial and stress. Jerry Falwell once stated that the greatness of a man is proportionate to his willingness to endure. A person who achieves greatness does so by strength of character. When others give up, he still presses on.

True greatness in a human being or in a movement must have all three: A worthy goal, a godly means to achieve the goal, and the will to endure to see it accomplished. When these three are present, this is a person whom God considers great.

The High Calling of Changing Nations

This brings us back to *why* we are making disciples of the nations. God is bringing to birth a great movement destined to affect the entire world. But this movement could be robbed of its anointing and power if we do not keep clearly focused on the *goals* God has for it. We must keep our hearts pure; we must persevere in godliness for the goal set before us. To be servants both of God and of people is a high and lofty calling. But it could easily degenerate, through the weakness of human flesh into:

. . . a Christian version of Moral Rearmament.

. . . a political cause that ends up dealing purely on a human and sensual plane. (This is what has happened to Western governments—the *why* has been lost for decades.)

. . . a modern-day version of the Crusades and the Inquisition that fought force with force and maligned the testimony of Jesus for centuries.

. . . a movement that has lost its center, and therefore, its power.

If ever a movement needed to consider deeply the heart and purpose of its calling, this one does. Why is God leading His Church into increasing leadership at this particular time? What are the goals in serving peoples and nations that God wants us to achieve?

I believe there are a number of things God has in mind for the reformation-oriented Church. Let's now look at them one by one, and determine to make them our own. Without them, greatness will elude us.

God's Glory Uplifted

The foremost goal of shaping nations must be for the glory and honor of God. This is the true end of all creation, that God might be seen as all in all. "For of Him and through Him and to Him are all things, to whom be glory forever. Amen" (Rom. 11:36).

The supreme goal of Christian reformation must be to give great honor, glory, credit, and praise to the God of the universe who alone is worthy of attention. He is the incomparable one who "inhabits eternity" and His glory is over all the earth (Ps. 57:5). Our motive must be to see our great God honored and praised among the nations. This is the language of the Psalms:

> Oh sing to the Lord a new song! Sing to the Lord all the earth. Sing to the Lord, bless his Name; Proclaim the good news of His salvation from day to day. Declare His glory among the nations, His wonders among all peoples.

> For the Lord is great, and greatly to be praised; He is to be feared above all gods. For all the gods of the peoples are idols, but the Lord made the heavens. Honor and majesty are before Him. Strength and beauty are in His sanctuary.

> Give to the Lord, O kindreds of the peoples, give to the Lord glory and strength. Give to the Lord the glory due His name; Bring an offering and come into His courts. Oh, worship the Lord in the beauty of holiness! Tremble before Him all the earth.

> Say among the nations, "the Lord reigns." (Ps. 96:1-10)

This must be the language of both our inner hearts and outer lives. *To God Be the Glory.* Any degree of awakening on the earth, any thing good and righteous among men comes from God. He will not share His glory with another, nor is anyone else worthy.

He is the author and fountain of righteous leadership. He is the originator and He is the stimulator. This is what we are to *shout* among the nations:

> Blessed be the Lord God, the God of Israel, who only does wondrous things! And blessed be His glorious Name forever! And let the whole earth be filled with His glory. (Ps. 72:18)

Let the whole earth be filled with His glory: This is the focus and work of Christian ministry. This is the supreme goal of human history: That God through Christ may share His love and all the earth be filled with the knowledge and glory of God.

As we seek to serve the nations, we must be ever so careful not to lift up men. We cannot be a movement built around human personalities. It is our pride and self-focus that so easily tarnish the glory of God. If the Church lifts up the glory of God in the nations, it must learn the secrets of humility and brokenness. Otherwise it will lack the authority and purity to carry it to the ends of the earth.

The fact is, the more we know about the plans and purposes of God, the humbler we should be. Knowing more about His plans for the earth should make Him bigger, and us much smaller. Yet as I Corinthians 8:1 teaches, often it works in the reverse as knowledge goes to our heads and we become arrogant and ego-oriented.

We must be radically committed to a walk of humility and purity before God. Our protection will be to lift up the glory and honor of the Great King in any and every situation. Isaiah writes,

Arise, shine; for your light has come, and the glory of the
Lord has risen upon you. For behold, darkness will cover
the earth, and deep darkness the peoples; but the Lord
will rise upon you, and His glory will appear upon you.
And nations will come to your light, and kings to the
brightness of your rising. (Isa. 60:1-3 NASB)

Notice that when the glory of God is your goal, nations
and kings will come to the "brightness of your rising." We
must not just talk about the glory of God, or assume that we
are working for His honor. We must consciously make His
glory and praise the motive of our hearts and the fruit upon
our lips.

God's Kingdom Extended

Another great goal of Christian reformation is that the
Kingdom of God be extended into all the reaches of the
earth. The primary message of Christendom is that the King
has come and His Kingdom is now being established among
all the peoples of the earth. The Kingdom and its King are
the center of reality. Bob Mumford tells us these facts about
the Kingdom of God. It is: ultimate—the sum of all good;
eternal—it will never end; absolute—it will not turn out
wrong; and infinite—it has no limit in time and space.

The Kingdom of God is the central message of the Bible.
God's plan for His Kingdom was given to King Nebuchadnezzar in a dream and interpreted by Daniel:

And in the days of those kings the God of heaven will set
up a kingdom which will never be destroyed, and that
kingdom will not be left for another people; it will crush
and put an end to all these kingdoms, but it will itself endure forever. (Dan. 2:44 NASB)

In the Old Testament days, God raised up Israel as a
prototype of the coming Great Kingdom of the Lord Jesus
Christ. One of Israel's greatest kings was David, who was
used to establish the kingdom of Israel in righteousness.

There are a number of interesting parallels between the temporal kingdom David established and the eternal Kingdom that Jesus secured.

First of all, in the case of both kingdoms, a friend who had become an enemy was killed or defeated. In David's life it was Saul who turned from God and become David's enemy. Before David's kingdom could be established, Saul had to die. In I Chronicles 10:13, 14, we read that God "killed him, and turned the kingdom to David the son of Jesse."

In the case of Christ's eternal Kingdom, the friend-turned-enemy was Lucifer. Lucifer was once a trusted archangel. Through pride he became the leader of a cosmic rebellion. On Calvary Jesus destroyed all the power of the evil one, paving the way for the worldwide establishment of the Kingdom of God (Col. 2:15).

The second parallel of both kingdoms is that after the defeat of the enemy, the king was clearly recognized and crowned. In David's case, this took place in the town of Hebron (I Chron. 11:1-3). In the case of Jesus, He was raised from the dead, and ascended into heaven to receive His crown (Eph. 1:20, 21). Can you imagine the welcome He received in heaven after being gone thirty years, returning to be crowned as the King of kings and Lord of lords?

Finally, David's kingdom required painstaking battle and the united effort of his followers to bring the land under his authority. When David became the new king, it was not an automatic transfer of power. It took many years "to turn the kingdom of Saul to him, according to the word of the Lord" (I Chron. 12:23).

This is also true of Christ's Kingdom. Satan was defeated on Calvary, but the world still lies under his grip, in bondage to sin. The work of the Church for over 2,000 years has been to unite as an army to bring the Kingdom of God into power in all the nations of the earth. Jesus' Kingship in the earth is not automatic. It has to be won through the work of a loyal and dedicated army.

The message Jesus Christ brought to earth was that the Kingdom of God had come (Mark 1:14, Matt. 3:2). He preached the Kingdom of God (Luke 4:43) and the majority of His teachings and parables were about life in that Kingdom. He said we must seek first the Kingdom of God (Matt. 6:33), and He said that one must be born again to see the Kingdom of God (John 3:3). He promised to reveal the mysteries of the Kingdom of Heaven (Matt. 13:11). He said He would give His Church the keys to the Kingdom of Heaven (Matt. 16:19). Jesus also sent His disciples out to preach the Kingdom of God (Luke 9:2). He said that the Kingdom of God was within us (Luke 17:21). And in His final days on the earth before ascending into heaven He "spoke of things pertaining to the Kingdom of God" (Acts 1:3).

The message of the Early Church was exactly the same. They went out into society and proclaimed the Kingdom of God (Acts 8:12, 19:8, 28:23). Christ's Kingdom was their central message, and their central love was the King Himself! They knew from the Bible that His Kingdom was destined to spread into all the earth, and as a loyal and united army they pushed its boundaries into all of the known world.

It is still our primary focus. The goal of Christian service and missions is the extension of the Kingdom of God. That's what it is, nothing else. All parts of teaching, revelation, and emphasis in the Church must be placed under the umbrella of the Kingdom of God. For our message to be biblical, clear, and rightly focused, each of us must set our hearts to go to battle for Christ and His Kingdom in the earth. That is the flag that we fight under. That is the government that we represent. Nothing else is worthy of our supreme attention.

The Bible never encourages us to preach the Church, because that would easily become focused on self and self-serving. We are told to *build* the Church and *preach* the Kingdom.

We need to examine our own hearts. Are we seeking *first* the Kingdom of God? Are we willing to serve that Kingdom in any way God chooses? Have we truly committed ourselves to the *army* of the Kingdom of God? If the answer is yes, God will allow us to participate in the glorious advance of His Kingdom.

God's Will Done On Earth

A third goal of servant leaders is for God's will to be done on earth as it is in heaven. This is a direct response to the prayer Jesus gave His disciples in Matthew 6:9, 10:

Pray, then, in this way: "Our Father who art in heaven, hallowed be Thy Name. Thy kingdom come. Thy will be done in earth as it is in heaven."

Notice that Jesus placed the will of God being done in the earth directly after the phrase "Thy kingdom come." He knew that when the Kingdom came in its fullness and power, it would then be possible for the will of God to be done on the earth. That Kingdom did come through His death and resurrection. The disciples then went forth to preach it, expecting God's will to be accomplished in all parts of the earth.

Their faith must have been greater than ours. Many Christians today do not believe God's will *can* be done on earth as it is in heaven. Most relegate that to a future kingdom in a new earth and a new heaven. But Jesus did not say that. He simply stated that once the Kingdom of God had come, it had the ability to bring the will of God into the affairs of men on earth. He did not say that this would be in perfection or finality. He just encouraged His disciples to believe in the greatness of the Father to bring His heavenly will into the earthly realm.

To what extent it will be accomplished in a fallen world, only God can tell. But at the least, every believer should live in conscious commitment to seeing God's will done in greater and greater ways in the governing of the earth. Isn't this what Jesus meant when He said:

You are the salt of the earth; but if the salt has become tasteless, how will it be made salty again? It is good for nothing anymore, except to be thrown out and trampled under foot by men. You are the light of the world. A city set on a hill cannot be hidden. Nor do men light a lamp and put it under the peck-measure, but on the lampstand; and it gives light to all who are in the house. Let your light shine before men in such a way that they may see your good works, and glorify your Father who is in heaven. (Matt. 5:13-16 NASB)

Jesus meant for His followers to enrich and enlighten the world as salt and light in their respective realms. Instead of leaving the world dark and tasteless, the Church was intended to live out the will of God among men.

And what is the will of God? The Bible uses this term in multitudes of ways, and with many shades of meaning. But one consistent point is: The will of God in heaven creates an atmosphere and society of perfect love, holiness, and righteousness. The will of God purifies according to His purity. This is why both Peter and Paul give us the following admonitions:

For you know what commandments we gave you through the Lord Jesus. For this is the will of God, your sanctification: that you should abstain from sexual immorality; that each of you know how to possess his own vessel in sanctification and honor. . . . For God did not call us to uncleanness, but in holiness. (I Thess. 4:2-7)

Therefore since Christ suffered for us in the flesh, arm yourselves also with the same mind, for he who has suffered in the flesh has ceased from sin, that he no longer should live the rest of his time in the flesh for the lusts of men, but for the will of God. (I Peter 4:1-2)

The will of God is for us to be holy and righteous. This is the essence of His being. For His "will to be done on earth as it is in heaven," His holiness must permeate the earth as it does the domain of heaven. This release of holiness and purifying power over sin is accomplished through the righteous living of the Church among the peoples of the earth. God's will is purity. The only purity a lost mankind can see and be affected by is the purity of God demonstrated in the lives of Christians.

A main goal of Christian servant leadership is to purify and clean up the earth. Believers should be taking their righteous acts into every realm of society, transforming them to resemble the will of God. The coming of the Kingdom means the coming of a new set of standards by which to live. The world operates by selfishness and lust; the Kingdom of God by "righteousness and peace and joy in the Holy Spirit" (Rom. 14:17). Christians should be continually elevating people and nations out of the lusts of the flesh and the defilement of sin. That's God's will.

When there is sin in the Church—scandal, sexual immorality, or corruption—then the Church is not doing the will of God, let alone guiding the world. We need to first get our own house in order. This is why a major purging is taking place in the Church as we move toward the end of the century. Only a purified Church can create greater righteousness in the world. This is the will of God and the marching orders for His people.

How can we be a part of the coming revival and reformation? By coming clean before God and then living for His will by helping to purify the world all around us. We must be particularly ruthless in the area of sexual sin. It is especially deceptive and corrupting to humanity. That is why it is mentioned specifically in the Scriptures already quoted.

Purity is the will of God. For you, and me, and for all of the sin-scarred world.

God's Bride Prepared

Another goal of God's Spirit today is to prepare the Church as His Bride to reign and rule with Him forever. One of the greatest mysteries is the glorious linkage between the Creator and us through the work of the Holy Spirit. This is pictured in the Bible as a marriage relationship, where Jesus is the Bridegroom and we are the Bride. And the Bible states quite clearly that the goal of this relationship is that of universal royalty: We are destined to reign and rule with Christ over the entire universe. Notice these utterly amazing words in Revelation:

> Worthy art Thou to take the book and to break its seals; for Thou wast slain, and didst purchase for God with Thy blood men from every tribe and tongue and people and nation. And Thou hast made them to be a kingdom and priests to our God; and they will reign upon the earth. (Rev. 5:9-10 NASB)

They will reign upon the earth. What a glorious statement about our destiny as the Body of Christ! We have been saved and transformed by the power of the Holy Spirit to one day help lead and govern one day the earth and all its affairs. Our calling is to cosmic leadership as royalty and family of the King! Revelation 20:6 reiterates this:

> Blessed and holy is he who has part in the first resurrection. Over such the second death has no power, but they shall be priests of God and of Christ, and shall reign with Him a thousand years.

Then in the last two chapters of Revelation we read about the new heaven and the new earth, and the Body of Christ, now pictured as the New Jerusalem, coming down from heaven, assuming her exalted position in the new order. In that amazing glimpse of the certainties to come, we read:

> And there shall no longer be any curse; and the throne of God and of the Lamb shall be in it, and His bond-servants shall serve Him; and they shall see His face, and His Name shall be on their foreheads. And there shall no longer be any night; and they shall not have need of the

light of a lamp nor the light of the sun, because the Lord God shall illumine them; and they shall reign forever and ever. (Rev. 22:3-5 NASB)

One of the goals of the plan of salvation was to raise up a people to their Savior who would participate in the leadership of the ages to come. As Paul Billheimer so wonderfully describes, the Body of Christ is *destined for the throne*. Rulership is a major part of the calling of the Church, not just in the world, but one day in the entire scope of the created universe.

Is it any wonder God is preparing His people for this ultimate calling of leadership? If we cannot learn to grow as servant leaders in society now, how can we ever expect to reign and rule in the supreme place of authority with Jesus one day? The calling of the Church is a calling to leadership. Right now we are being prepared for that very task.

Leadership is learned, it is not automatic. This is a very important time for us to develop, grow and mature. We must accept increasing responsibility in the nations of the earth. We need to submit to our Great King now and allow Him to fully prepare us for the destiny that lies ahead. This learning process will deepen and widen as the time for the fulfillment of God's ultimate plans approaches.

God's World Reached With The Gospel

Our final goal as servant leaders is to fulfill the Great Commission of our Lord to reach every creature with the Gospel. For nearly 2,000 years God has had this clear target: To have the Gospel presented to every person born. That goal is still unfulfilled. Lee Grady writes:

As we preach the Gospel, we must yield our lives to the Holy Spirit in order that the power of God can be demonstrated to the world. We must heal the sick, raise the dead, cleanse the lepers, cast out demons, and meet the needs that only the supernatural power of Christ in us can meet. If we do this, we can be assured that the Christian message will soon gain ascendancy in the world and become the predominant philosophy among the majority of the earth's population. When, and only when, this takes place will we have fulfilled the Great Commission.[2]

There are over five billion people in the world today, and they are multiplying at an astonishing rate. More than a quarter of the people on earth — over 1.3 billion — have never heard of Jesus Christ. Those 1.3 billion unevangelized people live in 223 geo-political countries. Not only have these people never heard of Christ — they are also *culturally distant* to the Gospel. In other words, even if every one of them had a radio or a television (which is not close to being true!) a language or cultural barrier would prevent their comprehending the reality of Jesus' death on Calvary. The job of the Church is to bridge that gap, and pave the way for all people to hear.

As we have already learned in Chapter Seven, Jesus commanded us in Matthew 28:19-20 to reach every *ethne* or people group, not just the 223 entities we normally refer to as nations. There are thousands of these *ethnes*. For example, China has thousands of ethnic nations within her geo-political borders, as does Russia and India. Most missions leaders agree that at least 16,000 people groups or *ethnes* are unreached.

World evangelization will not be accomplished until all of these 16,000 unreached peoples are presented the claims of Christ. Jesus said He would not return until this job was done (Matt. 24:14). Revelation 14:6 tells us that the eternal Gospel must be preached "to those who dwell on the earth — to every nation [*ethne*], tribe, tongue, and people." In Revelation 7:9 we are given a glimpse of the extent of Christ's salvation in the earth:

> After these things I looked, and behold, a great multitude which no one could number, of all nations, tribes, peoples [*ethne*], and tongues, standing before the throne and before the Lamb, clothed with white robes, with palm branches in their hands.

This Scripture explicitly says that some people from *every* nation, tribe, people, and tongue *will be saved* and worshipping before God's throne one day. That is nowhere near the case in the world in which we live today. Great inroads have been made for the Gospel worldwide. Over one billion people on the planet would identify themselves as Christians, making Christianity the world's largest single religious community. But billions of people, and thousands of nations and tribes have yet to be brought into the Kingdom of God.

That has always been the calling of the Church. It is what we were commissioned to do. It is still the one unfulfilled commandment.

World evangelization is the great *why* of the outpouring of God's Spirit on a human plane.

. . . *Why* does God want to revive an individual? To fill him with His Spirit to help reach other people for Jesus.

. . . *Why* does God desire to awaken whole churches? That they might help reach some of the 16,000 unreached people groups scattered around the globe.

. . . *Why* does God want to bring reformation to whole nations? So that they can send resources, people, and skills into all the earth to share the Gospel with others.

Nations that experience great revival and reformation are always in the forefront of world missions. Spiritual awakening produces freedom and prosperity that can be exported to other nations and peoples. This is one reason why the United States, despite all of her sins, has given so much leadership to world evangelism in this century. It is a nation that has experienced great revival, and biblical formation in her culture. That is why America has been a conduit of thousands of missionaries, billions of dollars, tons of resources, and tremendous missionary inspiration. But as Gary North points out, it is not limited to here:

Christianity was not invented in the United States; it was invented in heaven. The United States is only one of several "authorized distributors" of Christianity, and if its people cease to be faithful, this "distributorship" will pass to others entirely. It should be the goal of every Christian to see to it that he does all that he can to enable his nation to become one of these "distributors." This is what Christian missions is all about.[3]

A Great and Worthy Goal

If we are to participate in changing nations for Christ, then we must keep our hearts and lives pure, and focus all of our activities on the *whys* that come forth from the heart of God. We must place His glory above all else, stretch out the tent-pegs of His Kingdom everywhere, seek to establish His will on earth as it is done in heaven, prepare ourselves for leadership as the Bride of Christ, and be absolutely committed to the goal of total and complete world evangelization. Gary North summarizes it well when he says,

> There are now five billion people in the world. If we are to win our world (and these billions of souls) for Christ we must lift up the message of Christ by becoming the city on the hill. When the world sees the blessings by God upon a nation run by His principles, the mass conversion of whole nations to the kingdom of our Lord will be the most incredible in all of history. It will produce a social transformation that could dwarf the Reformation.[4]

This will take place for His glory, through His Kingdom, according to His will, through His Bride, and to achieve His goal of reaching all the earth with the Good News of Jesus Christ. If our motive, methods, and character are righteous before Him, then the movement of worldwide Christian awakening will attain to the stature of greatness.

But we must remember that there is only one type of leadership that true Christianity produces. There is one ultimate key to greatness in the Kingdom of God. It is the most difficult one, but it is the greatest and most necessary of all.

For Thought and Application

1. What are the three essential qualities of greatness? Name some historical figures who meet these qualifications. Name some others that the world esteems highly who do not meet these criteria.

2. Why is it important to focus on our goals and motives for changing nations for Christ? What will happen if we don't? Give some examples.

3. What are the five clear goals of Christian servant leadership in the nations of the world? Which is most important to you? How can you keep these in perspective in your own life and ministry?

4. Examine the goals and motives of your own life. Make sure they are in line with God's goals and principles of greatness. Set your heart afresh to seek first His Kingdom.

In this world the kings and great men order their slaves around and their slaves have no choice but to like it. But among you, the one who serves you best will be your leader. Out in the world the Master sits at the table and is served by his servants. But not here, for I am your servant.[1]

Jesus Christ

For though I am free from all men, I have made myself a servant to all that I might win the more.[2]

The Apostle Paul

TEN

SERVANT TO ALL

God is doing a wonderful work in the world today, and much of it centers around increased Christian compassion and servanthood in the nations of the world. Despite the dark storm clouds of sin and judgment that are also present, this emphasis on servant leadership is rising to the forefront because:

. . . There is a worldwide awakening taking place in the Church,

. . . The cause of world evangelization has risen to new urgency,

. . . and societal reformation is needed in many places to fulfill the Great Commission.

We have said that to make disciples of all nations is to teach the followers of Christ to live out their faith in all arenas of life—this could lead to the changing of whole nations. This can only take place when we live out a biblical Christian world view that brings redemption into every area of man's life. Because there are only two kingdoms in this fallen world, there are two types of leadership: The servant leadership of Christ through love and influence, or satanically-inspired domination through fear and control. God has called us to serve in both the spirit and methods of Jesus. He is our perfect example, and the source of all power and strength.

Societies contain many spheres of leadership ordained by God to bring freedom and harmony to human existence.

It is in these areas that future battles will be fought. It is a day of both revival and judgment, and out of the tension between these two, someone will emerge to lead.

We have also looked at questions that have a major bearing on Christian influence in society. What should we do in light of the Second Coming of Christ? Which philosophies or world views are the primary players in the battle for the hearts of men? Finally, we discussed the importance of the great goal of serving the nations for Christ: That God may be glorified in the fulfillment of the Great Commission in our day.

This leads us once again to the *absolute key* to Christian involvement in the nations of the world:

> What kind of leadership must the Church exercise in the world? What is the secret to seeing the lordship of Christ lifted up in the nations of the earth?

A Heart to Serve

The greatest need in the world today is for the Church to follow the example of her Lord and Master and serve the nations of the world better than anyone else. The ultimate key to leadership is the full manifestation of servanthood. The words of the Lord Jesus could not be simpler:

> But the greatest among you shall be your servant. (Matt. 23:11 NASB)

True greatness comes through serving others. There is no greater key — those who serve best are those who are worthy to lead. Notice once again the words of the world's greatest leader:

> In this world the kings and great men order their slaves around and their slaves have no choice but to like it. But among you, the one who serves you best will be your leader. Out in the world the Master sits at the table and is served by his servants. But not here, for I am your servant. (Luke 22:25-27 Living Bible)

The great challenge of the Church at the end of the twentieth century is whether she will rise to her appointed position in human affairs by assuming the place of the world's greatest servant. As Jesus so clearly stated, whoever serves people best will be given leadership and authority. This is an inescapable principle in the world God created. If atheists, or humanists, or Marxists, or humanitarians, or Moslems, or Hindus, or any other group serve their nations better than the Body of Christ, then they deserve to lead in those nations.

If there should be a race for supremacy in the world today, it should be in the area of serving, not armaments. If Christians learn to serve their cultures and peoples as Jesus would have them do, the world will see the greatest revolution ever. Leadership *will be* established through either servanthood or through slavery. The Apostle Paul said:

For though I am free from all men, I have made myself *a servant to all* [emphasis mine] that I might win the more. (I Cor. 9:19)

A Servant Leader

The word *serve* or *servant* is found some 1,452 times in the Bible. It is one of the largest topics of Scripture. (Remember, whatever God wants to emphasize, He says many times in Scripture.) Let's look at eight different characteristics of servant leadership in Scripture.

First of all, a servant leader must be humble. Only a humble person has been set free from the tyranny of ego and pride to see the needs of others. The more humble you are, the more significant other people become. Paul says in Philippians 2:3-4, that we should "do nothing from selfishness or empty conceit [pride and ego], but with humility of mind let each of you regard one another as more important than himself; do not merely look out for your own personal interests, but also for the interests of others" (NASB).

Christ produces humility in us when He saves us from ourselves. When we admit our selfishness, and turn to Him to be forgiven and changed, He empowers us to humbly reach out to others. We have been set free to humbly serve. Pride is a slave to ego; humility is a servant to Christ and to others. Pride leads to difficulties; humility produces freedom, and brings true leadership. Jesus said, "Whoever exalts himself will be abased, and he who humbles himself will be exalted" (Matt. 23:12).

Bob Mumford says we should never trust a man or a woman who doesn't limp. This refers to Jacob, who wrestled with an angel and came out limping, a broken and humble man (Gen. 32:24-31). You can see true humility in the broken and contrite spirit of a man or woman who has wrestled through selfishness and come out the other side. You can trust broken people the same way you can ride horses that have been broken.

Myron Augsburger, a Mennonite leader adds, "Servant leadership often means leading from our weaknesses, not using our strengths to hide behind lest our inadequacies be seen. Actually, our faith to move with our inadequacies makes possible the Spirit's dominant role."[3] The humble person will have authority to lead.

Secondly, a servant leader must be a man under authority. The New Testament has a word, *huperetes*, that stresses the role of the servant in relation to his superior. A true servant is not an independent soul—he has a clear line of authority under which he serves. To be a true servant one has to recognize masters, and operate in submission, counsel, and under control. You cannot be a Christian Lone Ranger and profess to be a servant. If you do not place yourself under the authority of others, you really are not under the authority of Christ.

If you have not learned to be a good follower, you are not qualified to be a good leader. Leaders who are not good followers almost always become tyrants. Rebellion and independence is within them, and this combined with egotism can be deadly. The true servant leader willfully places himself under the care and authority of others. This is easy because he is a broken man who knows the depravity of his own heart all too well. He gladly submits to others because he needs them to walk the pathway Christ has laid out for him. He appreciates authority for the protection it provides. The more humble he is, the more authorities he will recognize in many areas of life. His submission is a mark of his servanthood, and it automatically gives him the authority that others will want to follow.

A third characteristic of the servant leader is accountability. This is similar to being under authority, but the emphasis here is on what the servant accomplishes for the one he serves. A common word for this in the New Testament is the Greek word *doulos*. A *doulos* is a bond-servant who is aware of the stewardship entrusted to him by his master. The servant acts as a good steward with the overriding sense that he is accountable for his actions.

Jesus so graphically spoke of this in the Parable of the Talents. In that story, all of the servants *did* something with the money they were given. But only two of the three multiplied their stewardship with a keen sense of their master's expectations. This is the essence of true accountability. They did not settle for good or better—they set their sights on the best. They were rewarded for their servanthood, and the servant who settled for less had everything taken away.

If Christians are to serve the peoples of the world, we must know God's expectations and act accordingly. We must believe that we are accountable (not just encouraged) to make disciples of all nations and teach them all that Jesus commanded. We must accept as a stewardship the commandment of world evangelization. We must become accountable to being the best servants in the world, as well as the best stewards of our time, our money, our resources, and our people. We have a reason to do so—we must give account of ourselves to God.

Fourth, a servant leader must be zealous in his work. A servant works hard and does his work well. In the Scriptures, there is a Greek word that describes this—*diakonos*. The stress of the word is the goodness of a servant's work. There is no such thing as leadership without hard-earned labor. It is the hand of the diligent that rules [leads].

This is so basic. Most leadership is not glamourous. It's not a special privilege, nor a life of ease. It is just plain hard work, and those willing to pay the price gain authority by simply out-serving others. When you study the lives of great leaders in history, both inside the Church and in the world as a whole, you always find this quality of diligence in labor. Great servant leaders know what they want to do, what the needs of their people are, and then work to the bone to accomplish the task. They are exalted to leadership because they work harder for their cause than anybody else. A good servant leader combines a good cause with righteous methods and plain old hard work.

Most Marxist revolutions have been won through this quality of leadership, even if the righteous goal and godly means were missing. Vladimir Lenin brought the Bolsheviks to power in Russia in 1917 through tireless effort. He made himself a majority by working harder than the rest, and today much of the world is filled with atheistic communism because of his example.

We must be willing to work harder and more zealously than anyone else on the horizon. A servant leader gains influence by righteously winning the battle of labor. This is cultural conquest through hard work. There is no other formula for victory.

The fifth characteristic of servant leadership is steadiness and faithfulness of character. A true servant is quiet and dependable. They know that they have a job to do, and the master can always count on the job being done. A leader does not have to be flashy or have a dominant personality—but he does need to be steady, and totally trustworthy. When an employer finds a faithful worker, he tries to hang on to him with all his might. What usually happens is that the faithfulness of the employee is rewarded by increasing leadership and responsibility. This is what God thinks about the quality of faithfulness:

> No one who has a haughty look and an arrogant heart will I endure. My eyes will look upon the faithful of the land, that they may dwell with me; He who walks in a blameless way is the one who will minister to Me (Ps. 101:5, 6).

In a world that knows increasingly little about faithfulness and commitment, the Body of Christ has a golden opportunity to aspire to leadership in literally every dimension of life. One way in which Christians can give vastly needed servant leadership is to cultivate an outlook for steady, long-term growth and development. Most people today have lost the sense of working toward the future. With foresight and faithfulness of servanthood, the Church can give the world a beacon of hope. The present tumultuous time in history will cause people to look for leadership that is steady and firm. That leadership should be found in the Church of Jesus Christ.

Sixth, servant leaders love to work as part of a team. This flows out of their humility which values the gifts of other people. More and more the world is realizing that the best leadership is shared leadership. An awakened Church can offer the beauty of teamwork that comes from knowing God. M. Scott Peck, in his thought-provoking book *The Different Drum*, challenges world leaders to look to this important truth:

> The strength for real servant leadership can be found only when people work together in love and commitment. It can only exist in a climate in which leaders are emotionally sustained in community. It cannot exist in a climate of competitive isolation in which idealism and humaneness are crushed. Only through community will our officials be strong enough to truly be our leaders, truly to be peacemakers.[4]

True servant leadership has always been associated with teamwork. The best example of this is the cooperation of the Godhead who operate in different functions as Father, Son, and Holy Spirit, yet govern the Universe as One in the perfection of unity. This perfect model has been given to the Church and has resulted in the concept of plurality of leadership and teamwork in the Church.

The day of the super pastor, as well as the day of the super executive are coming to an end. Only in the strength of shared servant leadership can we cope with the immensities and complexities of life upon our planet. Here again, the Church has an amazing opportunity. But first it needs to follow the Head herself—then as a united team of servants, she can lead the world into greater fruitfulness and productivity.

Seventh, servant leadership is committed to developing the potential of others. A righteous leader is a true spiritual gold miner: He sees the gifts latent in the lives of others and wisely uses all means to extract and develop that gold. He knows success is not achieved through dominance, but through releasing the rich human deposits found in every man and woman made in the image of God. A high view of man is essential for good and lasting leadership. Christians should make the best leaders in the world because they respect the talents of others, given by the hand of their Creator.

In this area, the Christian world view towers over all others battling for supremacy on earth. Marxism and Islam share a low view of man and selectively suppress individual talent. Generally, they both crush initiative, creativity, and abilities. Talented people only want to escape their oppression, while the majority simply give up. Biblical Christianity is not threatened by the gifts and abilities of people: Rather, it is pleased to help propel them into their destinies.

A true servant leader will use power to release and elevate others. Dennis Peacocke wisely explains:

Power, or leadership, can go one of two ways. You can use it to make people or things do what you want them to do, or you can use it to draw God's purposes out of people or situations. . . . God views power as the ability to draw out of people and situations the purposes for which they were created. Servant leadership is just that; it serves by drawing out potential, helping turn it into achievement.[5]

And lastly, a servant leader does not care about position or status. This is contrary to his very nature. He exists to serve, and is motivated to do so out of the joy serving brings and the pleasure that comes to the heart of God. His is not the leadership of force or power. He has the leadership of loving influence and sacrifice. This humble quality is what gives him his true authority: He can be trusted to lead because he doesn't care about power.

Servants are not concerned about rank, privileges, titles, and benefits. A servant wants to give his life meeting the needs of others. If he can do that through a position of responsibility, that is fine. But if his position is taken away and given to someone else, that doesn't matter either. Nothing has changed in his heart. Titles and positions may be means to the end, but the goal of the servant leader is plainly and simply *to serve*.

A servant leader is easily spotted: If his position is taken away, he doesn't fight for it. And when it's given, he doesn't make a big deal about it. The servant leader is committed to serving God and serving people and leaves the authority and positioning to God.

The Bible is filled with examples of servanthood, and how service brings one into leadership. There are even four servant songs found in Isaiah 42, 49, 50, and 53. We should clothe ourselves in the teachings of servanthood from God's Word. There is an eternity to know about this awesome subject! There are many bright examples to show us the way.

The Good Example of David

One of my favorite leaders in the Bible is King David. Oh, he didn't start out as a king—but as a humble shepherd boy. But as he grew to love God and also to care about people, something very special began to set this young man apart.

David was called the "man after God's own heart." Certainly he will be seen one day as one of the greatest leaders of all time. What made David a great leader? Were the qualities of servant leadership present in his life?

An excellent book on the subject of servant leadership which we have briefly mentioned is *A Tale Of Three Kings* by Gene Edwards.[6] This powerful re-telling of the life of David shows him being trained in God's school of brokenness, first under the rule of King Saul, and later as he faced the rebellion of Absalom, his son, while he himself occupied the throne. Saul. David. Absalom. Of these Three Kings, two are governed by pride and power. Only one learned that true authority comes from humility and submission, found in the furnace of affliction.

One particular section of the book gives a vivid insight into how the servant leadership of David was formed. It was during the years when David was running for his life from King Saul. He was "wrestling with God and developing his limp." Gene Edwards tells it this way:

> These were David's darkest hours. You know them as his pre-king days, but he didn't. He assumed it was his lot forever. Suffering was giving birth. Humility was being born. By earthly measures he was a shattered man; by heaven's measure, a broken one.

> After long searching, some fugitives made contact with David. They had not seen him for a long time. The truth was that when they did see him again, they simply didn't recognize him. He had changed; his personality, his disposition, his total being had been altered. He talked less. He loved God more. He sang differently. They had

never heard these songs before. Some were lovely beyond words, but some could freeze the blood in your veins.

Those who found him and who decided to be his fellow fugitives were a sorry, worthless lot; thieves, liars, complainers, fault-finders, rebellious men with rebellious hearts. They were blind with hate. . . . They would have been troublemakers in paradise, if they ever could have gotten in.

David did not lead them. He did not share their attitudes. Yet unsolicited, they began to follow him. He never spoke to them of authority. He never spoke of submission; but to a man, they submitted. . . . Legalism is not a word found in the vocabulary of fugitives. Nonetheless, they cleaned up their outer lives. Gradually, their inward lives began to change too.

They didn't fear submission or authority; they didn't even think about the topic, much less discuss it. Then why did they follow him? They didn't, exactly. It was just that he was . . . well . . . David. That didn't need explanation.[7]

David had become a broken and humble man. That automatically made him a leader who was worthy of being followed. And he had become a servant of a gang of thieves and rebels! What followed was a life of godly leadership that revealed his understanding of authority, his sense of accountability, his many acts and zealous works for God, the faithfulness of his character and reign (except for the sins that revealed his humanity), his teamwork and shared leadership, his developing the potential of others, and his total disregard for position and status.

Put simply: David served God, sheep, a group of discontents, and eventually a nation. And he did so as a servant-leader who was blessed and exalted by God.

The Perfect Example of Jesus Christ

But the greatest example of leadership is the *perfect example* of servanthood found in the life of the Son of God, the Lord Jesus Christ. He was and is the greatest servant the world has ever seen. That's why He is also the world's greatest leader.

Servanthood and leadership always go hand-in-hand. Let's notice the correlation between servanthood and leadership that we find in the words of the Apostle Paul regarding Jesus:

> Have this attitude in yourselves which was also in Christ Jesus, who, although He existed in the form of God, did not regard equality with God a thing to be grasped, but emptied Himself, taking the form of a bond-servant, and being made in the likeness of men. And being found in appearance as a man, He humbled Himself by becoming obedient to the point of death, even death on a cross.
>
> Therefore also God highly exalted Him, and bestowed upon Him the name which is above every name, that at the name of Jesus every knee should bow, of those who are in heaven, and on the earth, and under the earth, and that every tongue should confess that Jesus Christ is Lord, to the glory of God the Father. (Phil. 2:5-11 NASB)

Jesus Christ, the God-Man, is the One who has forged a permanent link between servanthood and leadership as an example for all time. Philip Greenslade, himself a servant leader executive with AT&T for many years, shares in his excellent book, *Servant Leadership*:

> In a radical fashion Jesus, by example and word, establishes servanthood as the way in which his men are to lead others. He expressly repudiates every secular model of leadership in favor of servanthood. . . . It was the form of servanthood that the Son of God chose to pour His divine life into. And the Father didn't break the mold when He sent Him.[8]

The Lord Jesus demonstrated to perfection all the elements necessary for servant authority. He is not only the perfect example to us, but He is also the source of power to produce that servant leadership in us.

Jesus' servant leadership was perfectly manifested in His humility and brokenness of spirit. He was the most humble man who ever walked the earth. Paul says that we are to "have this attitude in ourselves which was also in Christ Jesus. . . . He humbled Himself." For most of us, it is usually the other way around. We do not choose to humble ourselves. God has to provide some circumstances to bring about the humbling!

Not so in the life of Jesus. He was totally humble in relation to God, to Himself, and in His relationships with others. He was able to truthfully describe Himself as humble in Matthew 11:28, 29:

> Come to Me, all who are weary and heavy-laden, and I will give you rest. Take my yoke upon you, and learn from Me, for I am gentle and humble in heart; and you shall find rest for your souls.

Few people would dare to make that statement about themselves, but Jesus did—because it was *perfectly true*.

He was also the most broken man that ever set foot on Planet Earth. But His brokenness was not due to wrestling over His own sin: It was a brokenness He carried over the sins of the world. Jesus was a man with a limp, but this was a part of His inner character, only proven, not produced by suffering and trial.

Jesus was perfect in accountability and submission to authority. He never acted independently or with insubordination. He was always under the authority and direction of God the Father. In being questioned about that authority in John 5, He remarked:

> Truly, truly, I say to you, the Son can do nothing of Himself, unless it is something He sees the Father doing; for whatever the Father does, these things the Son also does in like manner.

I can do nothing on My own initiative. As I hear, I judge; and My judgment is just; because I do not seek My own will, but the will of Him who sent Me. (John 5:19, 30 NASB)

One man who recognized the true submission and authority of Jesus was the Roman centurion described in Matthew 8 whose servant was paralyzed. What many people did not understand about faith, he quickly grasped—that faith and power are related to being under righteous authority. He said to Jesus, "I, too, am a man under authority. . . . Just say the word, and my servant will be healed." Jesus replied, "Truly I say to you, I have not found such great faith with anyone in Israel." He then spoke the word and the servant was healed.[9]

After walking in complete accountability all His life, Jesus was able to say at the end of His life: "I have glorified You on the earth. I have finished the work which You have given Me to do." (John 17:4)

True servant leadership always accomplishes its destiny and there is no greater example of this than the life of Jesus Christ.

Jesus' servant leadership was also characterized by His steady and faithful resolve. No man on earth has been busier with more responsibilities than Jesus during the three years of His ministry on earth. His schedule and lifestyle were simply exhausting! Crowds pressed around Him at all times, to the extent that He could no longer enter certain cities. He was so tired from serving and tending to the needs of others that He fell asleep in a boat that was encountering a huge storm. After ministering all day long, and not even having enough time to eat, He went up on a mountain and spent all night in prayer. He was constantly on the move, never really having a place to call His home. The book of Mark highlighted His constant activity by continually using the word *straightaway*: After Jesus did one thing, He would *straightaway* go on to something else. He had a goal to accomplish and a world to serve. He worked hard at that goal as no other man has.

And He did it with zeal. When the entrepreneurs of the day had defiled the temple by turning it into a marketplace, "He made a scourge of cords, and drove them all out of the temple. . . . His disciples remembered that it was written, 'Zeal for Thy house will consume Me' " (John 2:15, 17). No man was ever so passionate for the truth as Jesus Christ. He spoke with authority, acted with fervor, and served His Father with all His heart and soul and strength and mind.

Yet His activity and zeal did not take away from His faithfulness and control. He was steady and cool, always in haste but never in a hurry. People were drawn to Him—He was clearly on a divine mission, but always made time for them to feel accepted and loved. Jesus was faithful, ultimately, faithful unto death.

Jesus was the perfect example of a team-oriented leader, committed to bringing out the potential of His followers. The centerpiece of His strategy for redeeming the world was to gather around Himself a motley group of men and women who were nothing in the eyes of the world, but precious to the heart of God. His leadership of them, as Tom Sine points out, was:

> By telling stories, by inviting, by playing with kids, by giving away power, by washing feet, and by doing a lot of other things that are really counter to a power-oriented view of leadership. Most remarkably, He even lays down his life.[10]

He gave of Himself to them for three long years, walking with them, living among them, demonstrating His righteous life, and training them to be followers after His likeness.

He must have had his moments of wonderment! Would this team be able to take the Gospel into all the world? Fishermen and prostitutes, tax-collectors, and revolutionaries? With care and great skill, He released them into ministry.

His life was the message. His impartation to His team was the method. Carefully He drew out of all of them the elements of greatness, and when He left the earth, He sent them out to bear fruit.

Today over 1.7 billion people on this planet call themselves Christians because of His leadership and the power of His team. They were just ordinary people. But He was an extraordinary servant leader. He shared that leadership and authority with them. That lifted them up to be all that they could be.

And finally, the servant leadership of Jesus is seen in His total unconcern for position, status, or rank. That lesson He taught to His disciples in bold and living color:

> Jesus, knowing that the Father had given all things into His hands, and that He had come forth from God, and was going back to God, rose from supper, and laid aside His garments; and taking a towel, girded Himself about. Then He poured water into the basin, and began to wash the disciples' feet, and to wipe them with the towel with which He was girded. . . .
>
> And so when He had washed their feet, and taken His garments, and reclined at table again, He said to them, "Do you know what I have done to you? You call Me Teacher and Lord; and you are right; for so I am. If I then, the Lord and the Teacher, washed your feet, you also ought to wash one another's feet. For I gave you an example that you also should do as I did to you.
>
> Truly, truly I say to you, a slave is not greater than his master; neither one who is sent greater than the one who sent him. If you know these things, you are blessed if you do them." (John 13:3-17 NASB)

By that one act Jesus destroyed for all time any concept of leadership that smacks of power and position-grabbing. He had every reason to command both rank and status before His disciples. But He knew the essence of leadership: It is service to others. True leadership is measured by how many people you serve, not how many you control. By washing their feet, He showed His disciples the way God Himself leads the world.

He does it by serving. His followers are to do the same. He said that He gave us an example, and that we would be blessed to do likewise.

Servants to All

Certainly only God Himself can adequately lead us into the opportunities and challenges of the twenty-first century. In the end, it is His Sovereignty upon which we anchor our hope. Without His guidance and help, it will be a time of great temptation, of danger, and of difficulty. But He has chosen to extend His Kingdom through His Church—and that is why her response is so crucial to the world's future.

Every Christian must follow Jesus Christ by becoming a servant to all. Now is the moment in history to accept the challenge of changing nations through Christian servanthood. This is an *offensive* posture, not one of retreat. The strategy is nothing but the power of service.

The world is crying out for leaders to guide them. But no answers will work except those of the King of kings and Lord of lords. His is the pathway of obedience and servanthood. At this crucial juncture in human civilization, with a new century looming in front of us, this question paraphrased from Esther 4:14 asks the Church:

> Have we not come into the kingdom for such a time as this?

We must set our hearts on serving people and nations in the spirit and true servanthood of the Lord Jesus Christ. If we emphasize authority, we will end up in tyranny. If we properly emphasize serving God and serving people, we will give good leadership.

Will we try to lead by worldly means, or will we pay the price of serving people better than anyone else? There are short-cuts to power through manipulation and control. But the manner in which we gain power will also determine how we use that power—will it be by force and coercion, or by loving influence and servanthood? The cultural mandate of developing the earth is still the goal of God through His Church. Pat Robertson is right when he says:

> It is clear that God is saying, "I gave man dominion over the earth, but he lost it. Now I desire mature sons and daughters who will in My name exercise dominion over the earth and will subdue Satan, the unruly, and the rebellious. Take back my world from those who would loot it and abuse it. Rule as I would rule.[11]

The famous American frontiersman, Davy Crockett, said many years ago, "Be sure you're right, then go ahead." The need for servant leadership at this moment in human history is certainly the right path. The call of God to Christian servanthood is a trumpet blast too clear to miss or to ignore. But as G. K. Chesterton asserts, it all boils down to this:

> The Christian ideal, it is said, has not been tried and found wanting: No. Rather, it has been found difficult, and left untried.[12]

Leadership *will* be exercised in the world for the remaining days that God allots to man upon this fragile planet. Someone is going to give direction to the nations as we head into the twenty-first century. It could be the various forces of evil plunging entire peoples and nations into gross darkness and human despair.

But let our prayer and action be this: that the Bride of Christ may arise to her destiny, and give light and blessing to the peoples of the earth through serving them better than anyone else.

For Thought and Application

1. Why is true leadership exercised through serving? What happens when Christians do not serve their societies?

2. Name the eight characteristics of a servant leader. Which one of them really stands out to you? In which ones are you weak and in which ones are you strong?

3. What made David a good leader? During the failures of his life, what principles of good leadership did he violate?

4. Study the perfect servant leadership lifestyle of the Lord Jesus Christ (see Appendix—Jesus The Greatest Leader of Men). Set your heart to follow His example. Be filled with the Holy Spirit to be a nation-changer through the power of serving.

APPENDIX

JESUS, THE GREATEST LEADER OF MEN

The following description of the servant leadership of the Lord Jesus, by William MacDonald, is a measuring stick for our own methods and activities in light of the lifestyle of the world's greatest leader. If we are to truly serve people and nations, we must walk in the footsteps of the Master. These footsteps are clearly laid out below.

1. Jesus clearly envisioned the destination to which he was leading his people—the kingdom of God. The first principle of his leadership was that he knew precisely where he would lead the faithful and how to get there. Reversals and mid-course corrections were unnecessary under his leadership (Luke 9:51, 22:15, 16).

2. Jesus led without forcing his values on anyone or coercing anyone into following. That is, he never drafted anyone in violation of individual autonomy. Much prayer preceded the call of those who would be his closest colleagues in ministry (Luke 6:12, 13).

3. Jesus was not obsessed with gaining the psychological power of great numbers of warm bodies. Volunteers who would not pay the price of total commitment were turned away rather than being signed up on their own terms (Luke 9:57-62).

4. Jesus won the hearts of his followers by leading through friendship rather than fear. He shared with them his secrets and his strategy as rapidly as they could benefit from and implement them (Luke 18:26-30).

5. Jesus had no reason to hide his human finitude by impressive staging. Instead of barricading himself in inaccessibility (behind walls and many subordinates), he ate and slept with the troops, leaving them only for quiet times alone with his Father. Even little children had access to him (Luke 18:15-17).

6. Jesus was unafraid as all great leaders must be. The visible faces of clay could neither intimidate nor dissuade him from his objectives. Nor could the invisible powers of darkness deter him from accomplishing his mission (Luke 13:31-35).

7. Jesus never compromised his moral integrity in order to accomplish his objectives of his revolution. He operated above demeaning dirty tricks, back-door gifts, assassinations, rash unredeemable promises, or even flattery (Luke 11:52-54).

8. Jesus was patently selfless in his motives of leadership. He sought to bring believers to the depth of experience with his Father that he already enjoyed (Luke 10:22).

9. Instead of providing distracting entertainment for people to enable them to forget momentarily their confusion, guilt, suffering, loneliness, and unmet needs, Jesus provided solutions, corrections, and resources to meet those basic needs. The result for believers was a lasting foundation for joy (Luke 4:40-44, 9:37-43).

10. Jesus did not squander nature and its resources; he took control as Adam was told to do, taking "dominion" without wasting or polluting, in order to utilize nature to bless and help humanity (Luke 9:17).

11. Jesus, a forceful public speaker, could hold the attention of large gatherings without taking advantage of people. His speech was spiced with colorful, unforgettable sayings and illustrations. When facing large crowds, he did not become superheated and tyrannical. There were no harangues, but always with them there was a deepening

of his compassion. He gave clear and simple directions for finding one's way into the kingdom of God (Luke 5:1, 8:4-15, 13:22-30).

12. Jesus was appropriately tough or tender in dealing with everyone and every crisis. He gained the respect and loyalty of men and women alike. His leadership style of personal relationships fit the situation with just the right amount of pressure being exerted in every case.

13. Jesus never "pled poverty" for the kingdom of God, "took" offerings by psychological jerks, or extracted monies legalistically from the reluctant. But likewise he never did refuse people the privilege of giving who offered their gifts prompted by love (Luke 8:1-3).

14. Jesus' genuine wholesomeness was that of a man who was sure of himself. This made it possible for people to confidently put their faith in him and to gladly follow him. His winsomeness consisted of a perfect balance between self-assurance and affability (Luke 6:20-49).

15. Jesus was the concrete expression of what he taught (Luke 6:20-49). If one could not clearly understand where he was leading by what he was saying, he could find the same truths expressed and reinforced in Jesus' whole demeanor and activities. Those who were not abstract thinkers (four out of ten) could see the truth unfurled in his unforgettable actions and lifestyle (Luke 23:47).

16. Jesus was able to lead effectively and with full respect without the advantages of special identifying clothing and insignia that are universally recognized as symbols of authority. Royalty, the priesthood (Exodus 28:2), and the military must all step down to this leader dressed in ordinary clothes (and a special anointing) whose presence commanded respect wherever he was (Luke 4:18-22).

17. In decision-making, Jesus was neither indecisive nor rash. Prayerfulness was the fulcrum of his administration. Hence, the kingdom of God was never held back for want of resolute action, nor did it lurch forward on opportunistic whims and crash programs (Luke 6:12-16).

18. The power that Jesus tapped was not that whose source was in individuals; rather it was the power given him by God. This made it possible for him always to have something valuable to give freely to the people who followed him. (Most worldly leaders aggrandize power by first taking it from people, abrogating some of their rights and confiscating certain of their resources; and later in a display of paternalism they return some of what was previously taken.) Jesus did not need to do that for he depended heavily on divine resources to found the kingdom of God (Luke 3:22; cf. Acts 10:38).

19. Jesus was consistently resolute in that he followed through to the end with his goals for the kingdom. He would not surrender his aims for lesser ones when the going become difficult and his leadership was misunderstood. Thus he never backed off from the full-time responsibility of leadership (Luke 2:45-51).

20. Jesus knew well his followers and dealt with each one appropriately—not using the same patterns of assignment and expectation with such diverse men as Peter and John. He cultivated the development of the two-talent man and one twice as talented by giving each the proper resources and relationship in which to develop (John 21:17-22).

21. Jesus knew how to pace both himself and the revolution, sensing when to advance and when to withdraw from the crowds of people, when to refuel, and when to face up to his most trying hours. In the words of the Old Testament, he knew when and how "to go in and out among the people," and as a result his timing was never off (Luke 9:18-27, 19:28).

22. Jesus' settled concept of his own identity and of the one who sent him made his leadership rise above popularity. Therefore, he was psychologically impervious to popular praise of himself—it did not inflate him—and to negative criticism of himself—it did not deflate him. Knowing at all times what the Father thought of him gave great evenness and steadiness to his leadership (Lk. 4:22, 28, 29, 19:37-41).

23. Jesus had a uniquely positive revolutionary methodology (John 18:36):

   • not arms, but faith, hope and love

   • not explosives, but mountain-moving faith

   • not sabotage of the enemy, but doing good to those hating you

   • not fear, but the love that crowds out all fear

   • not crowd-pleasing propaganda, but the truth

   • not firing squads, but raising the dead

   • not deceit and intrigue, but parables, proverbs and enigmas

24. Jesus accomplished his revolution without dependence on the power structures of the world. He operated without any of the following standard foundations for kingdoms (Luke 20:1-8, 19-26):

   • institutional backing

   • political machines and party affiliation

   • government support or anti-government patriotism

   • class-struggle exploitation—playing on desires for upward mobility

25. Jesus met all of mankind's deepest needs—those that only the Creator and Savior of man can supply. Consequently, he is the only leader of all time that when

the deepest gratitude of followers wells up, and admiration calls for praise and exultation, it is not wrong to actually worship this leader as LORD AND GOD (Luke 24:52).

END NOTES

Introduction

1. Ron Boehme, *What About Jimmy Carter?* (Third Century Publishers, Washington, D.C., 1976).
2. On July 4, 1986 nearly three hundred Christian leaders, part of the Coalition on Revival, gathered on the steps of the Lincoln Memorial and called for reformation in the church.
3. Howard Snyder and Daniel Runyon, *Foresight*, (Nashville: Thomas Nelson, 1986) p. 70.
4. Ibid, p. 10.
5. Letter to the author dated March 7, 1988.
6. Philip Greenslade, *Leadership, Greatness, and Servanthood* (Minneapolis: Bethany House Publishers, 1984), p. 1.
7. Dr. Richard Halverson, *Cutting Edge* (Upland: Taylor University, April 1988).

Chapter 1—Make Disciples of All Nations

1. Matthew Henry, *Commentary on Matthew*. Matthew 28:19, p. 446.
2. Thomas Aquinas, *Summa Theologica*, Part I, Q. 103, Art. 3.
3. Ray Sutton, *That You May Prosper* (Tyler: Institute for Christian Economics, 1987), p. 125.
4. Allan Bloom, *The Closing of the American Mind* (New York: Simon and Schuster, 1987), p. 197.
5. Ibid, p. 204.
6. Jon Kennedy, *The Reformation of Journalism* (Wedge, 1972), p. 10.
7. Scott Peck, *The Different Drum* (New York: Simon and Schuster, 1987), p. 186.
8. Allan Bloom, *The Closing of the American Mind*, p. 40.
9. This theme is expounded on in, *Eternity In Their Hearts*, and in the personal experiences of the Richardsons as recorded in their first book, *Peace Child*, the story of their work among the Sawi tribe of Irian Jaya (Indonesia).
10. An excellent book on the subject of both the demands and freedoms of the Gospel within human cultures, is Paul Hiebert's *Anthropological Insights for Missionaries*.

11. Jon Kennedy, *The Reformation of Journalism*, p. 33.
12. Howard Snyder and Daniel Runyon, *Foresight*, p. 27.
13. This perspective is a revised version of an article written by Lee Grady entitled *A Vision For World Dominion*, pp. 4-11.
14. Bob and Rose Weiner, *Christian Dominion — The Legacy of Early America* (Gainesville: Maranatha Publications, 1985), p. 26.

Chapter 2 — A Kingdom World View

1. E. Stanley Jones, *The Unshakable Kingdom and The Unchanging Person* (Nashville: Abingdon, 1972), pp. 16, 21.
2. Richard Lovelace, *Dynamics of Spiritual Life*, p. 374.
3. Bernard Ramm, *Varieties of Christian Apologetics*, p. 180.
4. Abraham Kuyper, *Lectures On Calvinism* (Grand Rapids: 1931, 1975), p. 171.
5. Allan Bloom, *The Closing of the American Mind*, (This is the subtitle of the book).
6. Abraham Lincoln, as quoted in *Rebirth of a Nation* (Art DeMoss Foundation), p. 32.
7. Noah Webster, as quoted in *Rebirth of a Nation*, p. 33.
8. Ray Sutton, *That You May Prosper*, p. 278.
9. E. Stanley Jones, *The Unshakable Kingdom and The Unchanging Person*, p. 19.
10. Abraham Kuyper, *Lectures On Calvinism*, p. 189.

Chapter 3 — Two Kingdoms: Two Types of Leadership

1. Augustine, *City of God*, Book XIV:28.
2. Ray Allen, *The Washington Report*, July/August 1987.
3. Gary North, *Dominion and Common Grace* (Tyler: Institute for Christian Economics, 1987), p. 17.
4. E. Stanley Jones, *The Unshakable Kingdom and the Unchanging Person*, p. 15.
5. Ray Allen, *The Washington Report*, Vol. 4, No. 4.
6. Jonathan Edwards, *Work of Redemption*.

Chapter 4 — Serving: The Attitude of True Leadership

1. 2 Samuel 23:3
2. Proverbs 11:18, 19, 23
3. Luke 1:17
4. Allan Bloom, *The Closing of the American Mind*, p. 26.
5. Ted Koppel, *Commencement address*, Duke University, June 1987.
6. Gary DeMar, *Ruler of the Nations* (Ft. Worth: Dominion Press, 1987), p. 116.

7. Joy Dawson, *Intimate Friendship With God* (Old Tappan: Chosen Books, Fleming Revell, 1986), p. 69.
8. Gary North, *Dominion and Common Grace*, p. 113.
9. John Naisbitt, *Megatrends* (New York: Warner Books, 1982, 1984), p. 88.
10. Gary North, *Backward Christian Soldiers*, p. 47.
11. George Grant, *In The Shadow Of Plenty* (Ft. Worth: Dominion Press, and Thomas Nelson Inc., Nashville, TN: 1986), p. 154.
12. Allan Bloom, *The Closing of the American Mind*, p. 122.
13. Lee Grady, *Being Prophetic in a Right-wing, Left-wing Society* (Forerunner, March 1987).
14. George Grant, *In The Shadow Of Plenty*, p. 18.
15. Webster's 1828 Dictionary.
16. Robert K. Greenleaf, *Servant Leadership* (Ramsey: Paulist Press, 1977), pp. 62-66.
17. George Grant, *In The Shadow Of Plenty*, pp. 40, 45.

Chapter 5 — Stewardship: The Action of True Leadership

1. Isaiah 26:7, 9
2. Acts 10:35
3. Romans 6:13, 14, 16-18
4. Joy Dawson, *Intimate Friendship With God*, pp. 23, 42.
5. Lee Grady, *The Contest For World Dominion* (Gainesville: Maranatha Publications, 1985), p. 17.
6. Arthur F. Miller and Ralph T. Mattson, *The Truth About You* (Old Tappan: Fleming Revell, 1977), pp. 26, 27.
7. William Barclay, *The Gospel of Matthew* (1958), p. 280.
8. George Grant, *In The Shadow of Plenty*, pp. 50-55.
9. Most of these examples are taken from *In the Shadow of Plenty*.
10. Ibid, pp. 23, 24, 56, 110.
11. Ray Sutton, *That You May Prosper*, p. 218.
12. See Dennis Peacocke's excellent new book, *Winning The Battle For The Minds Of Men*.
13. Nate Krupp, message on The Great Commission, Virginia Beach, 1978.
14. Ray Sutton, *That You May Prosper*, p. 203.
15. Philip Greenslade, *Servant Leadership*, pp. 118, 119.

Chapter 6 — Changing a Nation

1. Abraham Kuyper, *Lectures On Calvinism*, pp. 29, 30.
2. Dooyeweerd, Herman, *Roots of Western Culture* (Wedge, 1979), p. 53. His perspective was predominantly the relationship between the spheres of church and state.
3. Bill Muehlenberg, *Abraham Kuyper* (Heidebeek Library Report No. 44, March 1983), p. 10.
4. Ibid, pp. 1-13.
5. Abraham Kuyper, *Lectures On Calvinism*, p. iii.

6. Ibid, p. vi.
7. Ibid, p. 94.
8. Ibid, p. 96.
9. Allan Bloom, *The Closing of the American Mind*, p. 57.
10. George Gilder in his excellent book *Wealth and Poverty* says, "Indeed, after work the second principle of upward mobility is the maintenance of monogamous marriage and family" (*Wealth and Poverty*, p. 69). Family is not only crucial to imparting values, but also vitally necessary for economic stability and growth.
11. A good treatise on this subject is George Grant's *In the Shadow of Plenty*, and also the popular work, *Losing Ground* by Charles Murray.
12. Abraham Kuyper, *Lectures On Calvinism*, pp. 82, 83, 93.
13. Robert Thoburn, *The Children Trap*, pp. 25, 26.
14. Austin Kiplinger, *The New American Boom*, pp. 5, 14.
15. Abraham Kuyper, *Lectures On Calvinism*, pp. 119, 130.
16. Abraham Kuyper, *Lectures On Calvinism*, p. 153.
17. Charles Finney, *Power From On High*, p. 68.
18. Abraham Kuyper, *Lectures On Calvinism*, p. 30.
19. Herman Dooyeweerd, *Roots of Western Culture*, pp. 48, 55.

Chapter 7—Occupy Until I Come

1. Charles Spurgeon, *The Treasury of David*, Volume IV:102.
2. George Ladd, *The Blessed Hope* (Grand Rapids: Eerdmans, 1956), p. 106.
3. E. Stanley Jones, *The Unshakable Kingdom and the Unchanging Person*.
4. Ibid, p. 18.
5. Gary North, *Backward Christian Soldiers*, pp. 32, 244.

Chapter 8—The Battle For World Leadership

1. As quoted by Lee Grady in *The Contest For World Dominion*, pp. 7, 8.
2. Abraham Kuyper, *Lectures On Calvinism*, p. 11.
3. Ray Sutton, *Who Owns The Family* (Ft. Worth: Dominion Press, 1986), p. 112.
4. James Reichley, *Religion In American Public Life* (Washington, D.C.: The Brookings Institute, 1985), p. 47.
5. Gary DeMar, *Ruler Of The Nations*, p. 151.
6. James Reichley, *Religion in American Public Life*, p. 48.
7. Karl Marx as quoted by Lee Grady in *The Contest For World Dominion*, p. 5.
8. Gary North, *Dominion and Common Grace*, pp. 227-229, and *Liberating Planet Earth*, p. 1.
9. Gary North, *Liberating Planet Earth*, p. 6.
10. David Aikman, *Pacific Rim* (Boston: Little, Brown & Co., 1986), p. 186.
11. Allan Bloom, *The Closing of the American Mind*, p. 196.

12. Austin Kiplinger, *The New American Boom*, pp. 71, 72.
13. Gary North, *Dominion and Common Grace*, pp. 231-232.
14. Abraham Kuyper, *Lectures On Calvinism*, p. 19.
15. E. Stanley Jones, *The Unshakable Kingdom and the Unchanging Person*, pp. 16, 17.

Chapter 9 — Goals And Greatness

1. Jonathan Edwards, *The Waterman Pamphlets*, vol.52:2, 1747, pp. 9, 10.
2. Lee Grady, *The Contest For World Dominion*, p. 17.
3. Gary North, *Liberating Planet Earth*, p. 12.
4. Gary North, *What Are The Biblical Blueprints?*.

Chapter 10 — Servant To All

1. Luke 22:25-27, Living Bible.
2. 1 Corinthians 9:19.
3. Letter to the author, February 18, 1988.
4. M. Scott Peck, *The Different Drum*, p. 324.
5. Dennis Peacocke, *The Bottom Line*, August 1987.
6. Gene Edwards, *A Tale Of Three Kings* (Augusta, Maine: Christian Books, 1980).
7. Ibid, pp. 31, 32.
8. Philip Greenslade, *Servant Leadership*, p. 3.
9. Story is found in Matthew 8:5-13.
10. Letter to the author, March 7, 1988.
11. Pat Robertson, *The Secret Kingdom* (New York: Bantam Books, 1984), p. 201.
12. G. K. Chesterton, *What's Wrong With The World?* Part I, Chap. 5, 1910, in *Bartlett's Familiar Quotations*, p. 742.

BIBLIOGRAPHY

Aikman, David. *Pacific Rim*. Boston: Little, Brown & Co., 1986.

Bahnsen, Greg. *By This Standard*. Tyler: Institute for Christian Economics, 1985.

Bellah, Robert. *Habits of the Heart*. New York: Harper & Row, 1985.

Bloom, Allan. *The Closing of the American Mind*. New York: Simon and Schuster, 1987.

Bright, Bill and Jenson, Ron, *Kingdoms at War*. San Bernardino: Here's Life Publishers, 1986

Bright, John. *The Kingdom of God*. Nashville: Abingdon Press, 1980.

Caird, George. *Principalities and Powers*. Oxford Press, 1956.

Chilton, David. *Paradise Restored*. Ft. Worth: Dominion Press, 1985.

Cunningham, Loren. *Winning, God's Way*. Seattle: Frontline Communications, 1988.

Dawson, Joy. *Intimate Friendship With God*. Old Tappan, NJ: Chosen Books, Fleming Revell, 1986.

Art DeMoss Foundation. *The Rebirth of a Nation*.

DeMar, Gary. *Ruler of the Nations*. Ft. Worth: Dominion Press, 1987.

Dooyeweerd, Herman. *Roots of Western Culture*. Wedge, 1979.

Edman, V. Raymond. *Finney Lives On*. Minneapolis: Bethany Fellowship, 1951.

Edwards, Gene. *A Tale of Three Kings*. Augusta: Christian Books, 1980.

Gilder, George. *Wealth and Poverty*. New York: Basic Books, 1981.

Grady, Lee. *The Contest For World Dominion*. Gainesville: Maranatha Publications, 1985.

——————. *A Vision For World Dominion*. Gainesville: Maranatha Publications, 1985.

Grant, George. *In The Shadow of Plenty*. Ft. Worth: Dominion Press, and Thomas Nelson Inc., Nashville, TN: 1986.

Greenleaf, Robert. *Servant Leadership*. Ramsey: Paulist Press, 1977.

Greenslade, Philip. *Leadership, Greatness and Servanthood*. Minneapolis: Bethany House Publishers, 1984.

Jones, E. Stanley. *The Unshakable Kingdom and The Unchanging Person*. Nashville: Abingdon, 1972

Kennedy, Jon. *The Reformation of Journalism*. Wedge, 1972.

Kraybill, Donald. *The Upside Down Kingdom*.

Kuyper, Abraham. *Lectures On Calvinism*. Grand Rapids: 1931, 1975.

Kiplinger, Austin. *The New American Boom*. Washington, D.C.: Kiplinger Washington Editors, Inc., 1986.

Ladd, George. *The Blessed Hope*. Grand Rapids: Eerdmans, 1956.

Lee, Nigel, *The Central Significance of Culture*.

McClung, Floyd. *The Father Heart Of God*. Eugene: Harvest House, 1985.

——————. *Father, Make Us One*. Eastbourne, E. Sussex: Kingsway Publications, 1987.

McDonald, Gordon. *Ordering Your Private World*. Nashville: Oliver-Nelson, 1984, 1985.

——————. *Restoring Your Spiritual Passion*. Nashville: Oliver-Nelson, 1986.

Miller, Arthur F. & Mattson, Ralph T. *The Truth About You*. Old Tappan, NJ: Fleming Revell, 1977.

Naisbitt, John. Megatrends. New York: Warner Books, 1982, 1984.

North, Gary. *Dominion and Common Grace*. Tyler: Institute for Christian Economics, 1987.

——————. *Healer of the Nations*. Ft. Worth: Dominion Press, 1987

Padilla, Rene. *Mission Between Times*.

Peck, M. Scott. *The Different Drum*. New York: Simon and Schuster, 1987.

Pippert, Becky. *Out of the Salt Shaker*. Downers Grove: InterVarsity Press, 1979.

Ravenhill, Leonard. *Revival, God's Way*. Minneapolis: Bethany House Publishers, 1986.

Reichley, A. James. *Religion in American Public Life*. Washington, DC: The Brookings Institute, 1985.

Robertson, Pat. *The Secret Kingdom*. New York: Bantam Books, 1984.

Schilder, Klaas. *Christ and Culture*. Winnipeg: Premier, 1947, 1977.

Sine, Tom. *Mustard Seed Conspiracy*. Waco: Word Books, 1984.

——————. *Why Settle For More and Miss the Best?* Waco: Word Books, 1987

Snyder, Howard and Runyon, Daniel. *Foresight*. Nashville: Thomas Nelson, 1986.

Snyder, Howard. *Kingdom Manifesto*.

Sproul, R. C. *Stronger Than Steel*. San Francisco: Harper and Row. 1980.

Sutton, Ray. *That You May Prosper*. Tyler: Institute for Christian Economics, 1987.

——————. *Who Owns The Family*. Ft. Worth: Dominion Press, 1986.

Thoburn, Robert. *The Children Trap*. Ft. Worth: Dominion Press, and Nashville: Thomas Nelson, Inc., 1986.

Weiner, Bob and Rose. *Christian Dominion — The Legacy of Early America*. Gainesville: Maranatha Publications, 1985.

ABOUT THE AUTHOR

Ron Boehme (pronounced BAY-mee) is an ordained minister who has served with Youth With A Mission for over 14 years. He is the founder of the YWAM work in Washington, D.C. and Virginia and has traveled to over 40 nations in an expanding teaching and preaching ministry.

In 1980 he served as the Capital City Coordinator of the Washington For Jesus rally which drew over 500,000 Christians to Washington, D.C. for a day of national repentance and prayer. In 1988 he served as the Executive Director of the Washington For Jesus International Delegations Committee, which brought foreign delegates from over 100 nations to participate in the gathering.

He is the author of one book, on the 1976 presidential elections (*What About Jimmy Carter?*, Third Century Publishers, Washington, D.C., 1976), and has various audio and video tape series on the subjects of leadership and spiritual renewal.

Ron currently works out of the YWAM National Office in Seattle, Washington, where he is the Director of the Revive America project. He and his wife Shirley, and their four children, make their home in Port Orchard, Washington.

You may purchase these books from the following distributors in your country:

USA
Frontline Communications
P.O. Box 55787
Seattle, Washington 98155
(206) 771-1153

AUSTRALIA
Christian Marketing
P.O. Box 154
North Geelong, VIC 3215
(052) 78-6100

CANADA
Scripture In Song
P.O. Box 550
Virgil, ONT LOS 1TO
(416) 468-4214

ENGLAND
Mannafest Books
13 Highfield Oval Rd.
Harpenden, Herts AL5 4BX
(05827) 65481

GERMANY
Youth With A Mission
Military Ministries
Mozart Str. 15
8901 Augsburg — Stadtbergen
(0821) 522659

HOLLAND
Pelgrim Intl. Boekenckm
Rijnstraat 12
6811 EV Arnheim

HONG KONG
Jensco, Ltd.
G.P.P Box 1987
3-3113768

NEW ZEALAND
Concord Distributors, Ltd.
Private Bag
Havelock North
(070) 778-161

SOUTH AFRICA
Mannafest Media
Private Bag X0018
Delmas 2210
(0157) 3317

RECOMMENDED BOOKS AND CASSETTES FROM YOUTH WITH A MISSION

Tape Albums by Loren Cunningham

● *Are there Answers,* an album of 6 audio cassettes ($24.95 US) Here Loren confronts and answers some of the basic questions asked today. Can you prove there is a God? Why the cross? Why do the innocent suffer? These tapes help you build your faith on understanding.

● *Let's Turn the World Around,* an album of 6 audio cassettes ($24.95 US) Solid teaching on walking out the Great Commission. These tapes present practical evangelism with God, a foundational teaching of YWAM.

YWAM Books:

● *Is that Really You, God?,* by Loren Cunningham ($6.95 US)
The story of a young man with a big dream. That dream was Youth With A Mission. Repeatedly, as Loren Cunningham worked to see his dream fulfilled through thousand of young people carrying the message of Jesus Christ to every Continent on the globe, he encountered opposition and difficulties. Often he was driven to his knees to question, "Is this dream really from you, God?" Seeing it become reality put Loren through some tough lessons - lessons that can help you learn to know the voice of God and run with the dream He has given you.

● *Anchor in the Storm,* by Helen Applegate ($6.95 US) The gripping true story of how Helen and her husband Ben, former captain of the mercy ship, M/V Anastasis, persevered through insurmountable odds to hold on to their dream to serve God on the high seas.

● *Before You Hit the Wall,* by Danny Lehmann ($6.95 US) Solid discipleship material. Danny lays out the basic training and the enjoyable disciplines that are foundational for a fruitful, ongoing walk with the Lord.

● *Daring to Live on the Edge: The Adventure of Faith and Finances,* by Loren Cunningham ($7.95 US)
A compelling, fresh look at the subject of faith and finances/ trust and provision by one of America's premier missions statesmen. This book will challenge and equip all who want to obey God's call, but who wonder where the money will come from.

● *The Father Heart of God,* by Floyd McClung ($6.95 US)
Floyd, Executive Director of YWAM, shares how to know God as a loving, caring Father and a healer of our hurts.

● *Intimate Friendship with God,* by Joy Dawson ($6.95 US)
Keys to knowing, obeying, and loving God by this dynamic teacher.

● *Leadership for the 21st Century,* by Ron Boehme ($8.95 US)
At the close of the century, how will you lead? A great book with the goal of changing the nations through the power of serving.

● *Learning to Love People You Don't Like,* by Floyd McClung ($6.95 US) Knowing that biblical unity is not always easy, this book shares keys for loving others, even when it is hard.

● *Living on the Devil's Doorstep,* by Floyd McClung ($8.95 US)
Join Floyd and his wife, Sally, in urban missions with YWAM, as they live and minister, first in a hippie hotel in Kabul, Afghanistan, and then next door to prostitutes, pimps, drug dealers, and homosexuals in Amsterdam Holland.

● *Personal Prayer Diary-Daily Planner,* ($12.95 US) What you get: quiet time journal, daily agenda, weekly goals, systematic Scripture readings, unreached people groups to pray for, prayer journal, concise teaching section, 9 pages of maps, and much more.

● *Taking Our Cities for God,* by John Dawson ($7.95 US)
New bestseller on how to break spiritual strongholds. John Dawson gives you the strategies and tactics for taking your cities.

● *Some of the Ways of God in Healing,* by Joy Dawson ($6.95 US) Do you have more questions than answers about healing? Joy is ruthless in her approach and pursuit of truth. This is a very enlightening book on the subject of healing.

● *Spiritual Warfare for Every Christian,* by Dean Sherman ($ 7.95 US) Spiritual Warfare is for everyone! It's more than rebuking demons. Dean delivers a no-nonsense, practical approach to living in victory.

● *Streetwise,* by John Goodfellow ($7.95 US) John thought he was finding freedom but he was actually walking deeper into a web of bondage. God had other plans for John and showed him how to walk in real freedom.

● *Walls of My Heart,* by Dr. Bruce Thompson ($8.95 US) Dr. Bruce's popular teaching, now in book form, deals with the wounds and hurts that we all receive, and how to receive biblical healing.

● *We Cannot but Tell,* by Ross Tooley ($6.95 US) How to evangelize with love and compassion. Great for group studies as well as personal growth. Learn to reach out from your heart.

● *Winning, God's Way,* by Loren Cunningham ($6.95 US) Winning Comes through laying down your life. This book gives the reader a look at the Cunningham's personal struggles and victories. A classic teaching of YWAM.

For a complete catalog of books and cassettes, write to the address below. To order any of the above listed books, write the title and quantity desired and send with the amount in US dollars.

FREE shipping at book rate with your order from this book.

YWAM Publishing
P.O. Box 55787
Seattle, WA 98155 USA
tel. (206) 771-1153